BEING
GOD'S
FRIEND

BEING GOD'S FRIEND

CHARLES SPURGEON

[W] *Whitaker House*

Unless otherwise indicated, all Scripture quotations are taken from the *King James Version* (KJV) of the Bible.

Scripture quotations marked (RV) are taken from the *Revised Version* of the Holy Bible.

BEING GOD'S FRIEND

ISBN: 0-88368-381-4
Printed in the United States of America
Copyright © 1997 by Whitaker House

Whitaker House
30 Hunt Valley Circle
New Kensington, PA 15068

3 4 5 6 7 8 9 10 11 12 / 07 06 05 04 03 02 01 00 99

Contents

Chapter 1

The Obedience of Faith

*By faith Abraham, when he was called to go out
into a place which he should after receive for an
inheritance, obeyed; and he went out, not
knowing whither he went.*
—Hebrews 11:8

O bedience—what a blessing it would be if
we were all trained to it by the Holy
Spirit! If we were perfectly obedient, we
would be fully restored. If the whole world
would obey the Lord, it would be heaven on
earth. Perfect obedience to God would mean
love among men, justice to all classes, and
peace in every land. Our wills bring envy,
malice, war. But if we would only obey the
Lord's will, we would receive love, joy, rest,
bliss. Obedience—let us pray for it for ourselves and others!

> Is there a heart that will not bend
>   To thy divine control?
> Descend, O sovereign love, descend,
>   And melt that stubborn soul!

I want to emphasize part of the verse from Hebrews 11 that starts this chapter: *"By faith Abraham...obeyed."* It is certainly true that although we have had to mourn our disobedience with many tears and sighs, we now find joy in yielding ourselves as servants of the Lord: our deepest desire is to do the Lord's will in all things. Oh, for obedience! It has been supposed by many badly instructed people that the doctrine of justification by faith is opposed to the teaching of good works, or obedience. There is no truth in the supposition. We who believe in justification by faith teach the obedience of faith.

Faith is the fountain, the foundation, and the fosterer of obedience. Men do not obey God until they believe Him. We preach faith so that men may be brought to obedience. To disbelieve is to disobey. One of the first signs of practical obedience is found in the obedience of the mind, the understanding, and the heart; and this is expressed in believing the teaching of Christ, trusting in His work, and resting in His salvation. Faith is the morning star of obedience. If we want to work the work of God, we must believe on Jesus Christ whom He has sent.

Beloved, we do not give a secondary place to obedience, as some suppose. We look on the obedience of the heart to the will of God as salvation. The attainment of perfect obedience would mean perfect salvation. We regard sanctification, or obedience, as the great purpose for which the Savior died. He shed His blood so that He might cleanse us from dead works, and purify unto Himself a people *"zealous of good works"* (Titus 2:14).

It is for this that we were chosen: we are *"elect unto obedience"* (1 Pet. 1:2) and holiness. We know nothing of an election in which we would continue in sin. It is for this that we have been called: we are *"called to be saints"* (Rom. 1:7). Obedience is the principal objective of the work of grace in the hearts of those who are chosen and called. We are to become obedient children, conformed to the image of Jesus, our Elder Brother, with whom the Father is *"well pleased"* (Matt. 3:17).

The Obedience That Comes from Faith

The obedience that comes from faith is a noble obedience. The obedience of a slave ranks only a little higher than the obedience of a well-trained horse or dog, for it is tuned to the crack of the whip. Obedience that is not cheerfully rendered is not the obedience of the heart, and, consequently, is of little worth before God. If a person obeys because he has no choice in the matter, and would rebel if he had the opportunity, there is nothing in his obedience. The obedience of faith springs from an internal principle and not from external compulsion. It is sustained by the mind's most sober reasoning and the heart's warmest passion.

It happens in this way: A person reasons with himself that he ought to obey his Redeemer, his Father, his God; and, at the same time, the love of Christ constrains him to do so. Therefore, what argument suggests, affection performs. A sense of great obligation, an understanding of the justness of obedience, and a spiritual renewal of the heart produce an obedience that becomes essential to the sanctified soul. Therefore, he is not relaxed in the time of temptation or destroyed in the hour of losses and sufferings. There is no trial of life that can turn the gracious soul from his passion for obedience, and death itself will only enable him to render an obedience that will be as blissful as it will be complete. A chief ingredient of heaven is that we will see the face of our Lord and *"serve him day and night in his temple"* (Rev. 7:15).

Meanwhile, the more fully we obey while we are still on earth, the nearer we will be to His temple gate. May the Holy Spirit work in us, so that, by faith—like Abraham—we may obey!

The Obedience of a Child

I am writing to you about absolute obedience to the Lord God. Yet, I am referring to the obedience of a child, not the obedience of a slave; the obedience of love, not of terror; the obedience of faith, not of dread. As God helps me, I will urge you to seek a stronger faith so that you may reach this obedience. *"By faith Abraham...obeyed."* In every case where the father of the faithful obeyed, it was the result of his faith. And in every case in which you and I will render true obedience, it will be the product of our faith.

Obedience that God can accept never comes out of a heart that thinks that God is a liar. It is worked in us by the Spirit of the Lord, through our belief in the truth, love, and grace of our God in Christ Jesus. If you are currently being disobedient, or have been so, the road to a better state of things is trust in God. You cannot hope to render obedience by merely forcing your conduct into a certain groove or by unaided, determined effort. There is a free-grace road to obedience, and that is receiving, by faith, the Lord Jesus, who is the gift of God, and who *"of God is made unto us...sanctification"* (1 Cor. 1:30).

We accept the Lord Jesus by faith, and He teaches us obedience, and creates it in us. The more faith in Him that you have, the more obedience to Him you will manifest. Obedience naturally flows out of faith, *"for as* [a man] *thinketh in his heart, so is he"* (Prov. 23:7); and the holy obedience of a person's life will be in proportion to the strength and purity of his faith in God, as He is revealed in Christ Jesus.

So that we can best understand how to apply these truths to our lives, let us consider several important aspects of obedience to God: the kind of faith that produces obedience, the kind of obedience that faith produces, and the kind of life that comes out of this faith and obedience. Let us trust the Holy Spirit for His gracious illumination.

Faith That Produces Obedience

Beloved in the Lord, we know that He is sovereign, and that His will is law. We feel that God, our Maker, our Preserver, our Redeemer, and our Father, should have our unswerving service. We unite, also, in confessing that we are not our own, for we are bought with a price (1 Cor. 6:19–20). The Lord our God has a right to us that we would not wish to question. He has a greater claim on our fervent service than He has on the services of angels, for, while they were created as we have been, still they have never been redeemed by precious blood.

Faith in God's Right to Command

Faith that produces obedience is therefore faith in God and His right to command our obedience. Our glorious, incarnate God has an unquestioned right to every breath we breathe, to every thought we think, to every moment of our lives, and to every capacity of our being. We believe that it is right and just that Jehovah is our Lawgiver and our Ruler. This loyalty of our minds is based on faith and is a chief factor that persuades us to obey. Always cultivate this feeling. The Lord is our Father, but He is *our Father which art in heaven*" (Matt. 6:9). He draws near to us in condescension; but it is condescension, and we must not presume to think of Him as though He were like us.

There is a holy familiarity with God that cannot be enjoyed too much, but there is a flippant familiarity with God that cannot be abhorred too much. The Lord is King; His will

is not to be questioned; His every word is law.
Let us never question His sovereign right to
decree what He pleases and to fulfill the decree, to command what He pleases and to
punish every shortcoming. Because we have
faith in God as Lord of all, we gladly pay Him
our homage, and we desire in all things to say,
"Thy will be done in earth, as it is in heaven"
(Matt. 6:10).

Faith in the Justness of God's Commands

Next, we must have faith in the rightness of
all that God says or does. I hope that you do not
think of God's sovereignty as tyranny or imagine that He ever could or would will anything
except what is right. Neither should we admit
into our minds a suspicion that the Word of God
is incorrect in any matter whatever, as though
the Lord Himself could err. We will not have it
that God, in His Holy Book, makes mistakes
about matters of history or science anymore
than He does about the great truths of salvation. If the Lord is God, He must be infallible;
and if He can be described as being in error in
the little respects of human history and science,
He cannot be trusted in the greater matters.

Beloved, Jehovah never errs in deed or in
word. And when we find His law written either

in the Ten Commandments or anywhere else, we believe that there is not a precept too many or too few. Whatever the precepts of the law or the Gospel may be, they are pure and altogether holy. The words of the Lord are like *"fine gold"* (Ps. 19:10), pure, precious, and weighty—not one of them may be neglected.

We hear people talking about "minor points of the law" and so on. However, we must not consider any word of our God as a minor thing, if by that expression it is implied that it is of small importance. We must accept every single word of precept or prohibition or instruction as being what it ought to be, neither to be diminished nor increased. We should not reason about the command of God as though it might be set aside or amended. He commands: we obey. May we enter into that true spirit of obedience, which is the unshakable belief that the Lord is right! Nothing short of this is the obedience of the inner man—the obedience that the Lord desires.

Faith in Our Personal Obligation to Obey

Furthermore, we must have faith in the Lord's call upon us to obey. Abraham went out from his father's house because he felt that, whatever God may have said to others, He had spoken to him and said, *"Get thee out of thy country, and from thy kindred, and from thy father's house, unto a land that I will show thee"* (Gen. 12:1). Whatever the Lord may have said to the Chaldeans or to other families in Ur, Abraham was not so much concerned with that as with the special word of command that the Lord had sent to his own soul.

Oh, if only we were earnest to render personal obedience most of all! It is very easy to offer to God a sort of "other people's obedience"—to imagine that we are serving God when we are finding fault with our neighbors and complaining that they are not as godly as they ought to be. It is true that we cannot help seeing their shortcomings, but we would do well to be less observant of these shortcomings than we are. Let us turn our magnifying glasses on ourselves. It is not so much our business to be weeding other people's gardens as it is to be keeping our own vineyards. Each person should pray, *"Lord, what wilt thou have me to do?"* (Acts 9:6).

We who are His chosen, redeemed from among men, and called out from the rest of mankind, ought to feel that if no other ears hear the divine call, our ears must hear it; and if no other hearts obey, our souls rejoice to do so. The apostle Paul wrote that we are to present ourselves to God as *"a living sacrifice, holy, acceptable unto God, which is* [our] *reasonable service"* (Rom. 12:1). The strongest ties of gratitude hold us to the service of Jesus. We must be obedient in life to Him who, for our sakes, was obedient unto death (Phil. 2:8).

Our service to our Lord is freedom. We want to yield to His will. To delight Him is our delight. It is a blessed thing when the inmost nature yearns to obey God, when obedience grows into a habit and becomes the very element in which the spirit breathes. Surely this should be the case with every one of the blood-washed children of the Most High, and their lives will prove that it is so. Others are also bound to obey, but we should attend most to our own personal obligations and set our own houses in order. Obedience should begin at home, and it will find its hands full enough there.

Faith That Is Our Chief Authority

Genuine obedience arises out of a faith that is the chief authority over all our actions. The kind of faith that produces obedience is lord of the understanding; it is a royal faith. The true believer believes in God more than he believes in anything else and everything else. He can say, *"Let God be true, but every man a liar"* (Rom. 3:4). His faith in God has become the crown of all his belief, the most assured of all his confidences.

As gold is to inferior metals, so is our trust in God to all our other trusts. To the genuine believer, the eternal is as much above the temporal as the heavens are above the earth. The infinite rolls, like Noah's flood, over the tops of the hills of the present and the finite. If a truth is infused with the glory of God, the believer will value it. However, if God and eternity are not in it, he will leave trifles to those who choose them. You must have a paramount faith in God, or else the will of God will not be a sovereign rule to you. Only a reigning faith will make us subject to its power, so that we will be obedient to the Lord in all things.

The chief thought in life with the true believer is: How can I obey God? His greatest concern is to do the will of God, or to yield to that will in a way that is pleasing to God. And if he can obey, he will not negotiate with God or be distracted with any reservations on his part. He will pray, "Refine me from the dross of rebellion, and let the furnace be as fierce as you will." His choice is neither wealth nor ease nor honor, but that he may glorify God in his body, and in his spirit, which are God's (1 Cor. 6:20). Obedience has become as much his rule as self-will is the rule of others. His cry to the Lord is, "By your command I stay or go. Your will is my will; Your pleasure is my pleasure; Your law is my love."

May God grant us a supreme, overmastering faith, for this is the kind of faith that we must have if we are to lead obedient lives. We must have faith in God's right to rule, faith in the justness of His commands, faith in our personal obligation to obey, and faith that His commands must be the chief authority of our lives. With the faith that belongs to God's elect, we will realize the object of our election, namely, *"that we should be holy and without blame before him in love"* (Eph. 1:4).

Faith in Action

Dear friend, do you have this kind of faith? I will withdraw the question and ask it of myself: Do I have that faith that leads me to obey my God? For, obedience, if it is the kind of which we are speaking, is faith in action—faith walking with God, or, shall I say, walking *"before the LORD in the land of the living"* (Ps. 116:9)? If we have a faith that is greedy in hearing, severe in judging, and rapid in self-congratulation, but not inclined to obedience, we have the faith of hypocrites. If our faith enables us to set ourselves up as patterns of

sound doctrine and qualifies us to crack the
heads of all who differ from us, yet lacks the
fruit of obedience, it will leave us among the
"dogs" mentioned in the book of Revelation,
who are outside the city of God.

The only faith that distinguishes the children of God is the faith that makes us obey. It
is better to have the faith that obeys than the
faith that moves mountains. I would rather
have the faith that obeys than the faith that
heaps the altar of God with sacrifices and per-
fumes His courts with incense. I would rather
obey God than rule an empire. For, after all,
the loftiest sovereignty a soul can inherit is to
have dominion over self by rendering believing
obedience to the Most High. Therefore, this is
the kind of faith we need: *"By faith Abraham...obeyed."* The only way you and I can
obey is by faith alone.

The Obedience That Faith Produces

Let us now consider the kind of obedience
that faith produces. I will illustrate this by
what we can learn from taking the verse as a
whole.

Immediate Obedience

Genuine faith in God creates a prompt
obedience. *"By faith Abraham, when he was*

called to go out into a place which he should after receive for an inheritance, obeyed." Abraham immediately responded to the command. Delayed obedience is disobedience. I wish some Christians who put off duty would remember this. Continued delay of duty is a continuous sin. If I do not obey the divine command, I sin; and every moment that I continue in that condition, I repeat the sin. This is a serious matter. If a certain act is my duty at this hour, and I leave it undone, I have sinned. But it will be equally incumbent upon me during the next hour, and if I still refuse, I disobey again, and so on, until I do obey.

Neglect of a standing command must grow very grievous if it is persisted in for years. To the extent that the conscience becomes callous on the subject, the guilt becomes even more provoking to the Lord in proportion. To refuse to do right is a great evil. However, it is far worse to continue in that refusal until the conscience grows numb on the matter.

I remember a person who came to be baptized. He said that he had been a believer in the Lord Jesus for forty years and had always believed that the ordinance was scriptural. I felt grieved that he had been disobedient to a known duty for so long, and I proposed to him that he should be baptized at once. It was in a village, and he said that there was no place convenient for it. I offered to go with him to the brook and baptize him, but he said, "No, *'he that believeth shall not make haste'*" (Isa. 28:16).

Here was someone who had willfully disobeyed his Lord for as many years as the Israelites were in the wilderness, in a matter that was very easy to fulfill. Yet, after confessing his fault, he was not willing to amend it, but perverted a passage of Scripture to excuse himself in further delay. David said, *"I made haste, and delayed not to keep thy commandments"* (Ps. 119:60). I give this case as a typical illustration; there are a hundred spiritual, moral, domestic, business, and religious duties that men put off in the same manner, as if they thought that any time would do for God and that He must take His turn with the rest.

What would you say to your son if you told him to go on an errand, and he answered you, "I will go tomorrow." Surely, you would give him "tomorrow" in a way that he would not soon forget. Your tone would be sharp, and you would tell him to go at once. If he then promised to go in an hour, would you call that obedience? It would be impudence. Obedience is for the present tense; it must be prompt, or it is nothing. Obedience respects the time of the command as much as any other part of it. To hesitate is to be disloyal. To stop and consider whether or not you will obey is rebellion in the seed. If you believe in the living God for eternal life, you will be quick to do your Lord's commands, even as a maid obeys her mistress. You will not be like a horse, which needs whip and spur. Your love will do more for you than compulsion could do for slaves. You will have wings on your heels to speed you along the way of obedience. *"To day if ye will hear his voice, harden not your heart"* (Ps. 95:7–8).

Exact Obedience

Next, obedience should be exact. Even Abraham's obedience failed somewhat in this at first. He started at once from Ur of the Chaldees, but he only went as far as Haran, and he stayed there until his father died. Then the command came to him again, and he set off for the land that the Lord had promised to show him. If you have only half obeyed, I pray that you may pay close attention to this. Do all that the Lord commands and be very careful not to withhold any part of the revenue of obedience.

Yet, the great Patriarch's error was soon corrected, for we read that *"Abraham, when he*

was called to go out...went out." I have only
omitted intermediate words, which do not alter
the meaning. This is exactly how we should
obey. We should do what the Lord commands—just that, and not another thing of our
own devising.

It is very interesting how people try to
give God something other than what He asks
for! The Lord says, *"My son, give me thine
heart"* (Prov. 23:26), and they give Him ceremonies. He asks for obedience, and they give
Him man-made religion. He asks for faith and
love and justice, and they offer meaningless
sacrifices. They will give everything except the
one thing that He will be pleased with: *"To
obey is better than sacrifice, and to hearken
than the fat of rams"* (1 Sam. 15:22).

If the Lord has given you true faith in
Himself, you will not be concerned so much
about doing a notable thing as about doing exactly what God would have you to do. Pay attention to even the smallest parts of the Lord's
precepts. Attention to little things is a fine fea-
ture of obedience. The essence of obedience lies
much more in the little things than in the
great ones. Few dare to rush into great crimes,
and yet people will indulge in secret rebellion,
for their hearts are not right with God. Therefore, too many mar what they call obedience by

forgetting that they serve a God who searches the heart and tries the mind, who observes thoughts and motives. He wants us to obey Him with the heart. This will lead us not merely to regard a few pleasing commands, but also to have respect for His entire will. Oh, for a tender conscience that will not willfully neglect or presumptuously transgress!

Practical Obedience

And next, make a special note of the fact that Abraham rendered practical obedience. When the Lord commanded Abraham to leave his father's house, he did not say that he would think it over; he did not discuss the pros and cons in an essay; he did not ask his father, Terah, and his neighbors to consider it. Rather, as he was called to go out, he went out. Dear friends, we have so much talk and so little obedience! The religion of mere brain and jaw does not amount to much. We lack the religion of hands and feet.

I remember a place in Yorkshire, England, where, years ago, a good man said to me, "We have a real good minister." I said, "I am glad to hear it." "Yes," he said, "he is a fellow who preaches with his feet." Well, now, it is an excellent thing if a preacher preaches with his feet by walking with God and with his hands by working for God. A person does well if he glorifies God by where he goes and by what he does. He will surpass fifty others who only preach religion with their tongues. You, dear readers, are not good hearers as long as you are only hearers. But when the heart is affected by the ear and the hand follows the heart, then your faith is proved. That kind of obedience, which comes from faith in God, is real obedience, since it shows itself by its works.

Farseeing Obedience

Moreover, faith produces a farseeing obedience. Note this: *"Abraham, when he was called to go out into a place which he should after receive for an inheritance."* How many people would obey God if they were paid for it on the spot! They have *"respect unto the recompense of the reward"* (Heb. 11:26), but they must have it in the palms of their hands. With them, "A bird in hand is better far, than two which in the bushes are." When they are told that there is heaven to be gained, they answer that, if heaven were to be had here, as an immediate freehold, they might attend to it, but they cannot afford to wait. To inherit a country after this life is over is too much like a fairy tale for their practical minds.

There are many who inquire: Will religion pay? Is there anything to be made out of it? Will I have to close my shop on Sundays? Must I alter the way I do business, and curtail my profits? When they have totaled up the cost and have taken all things into consideration, they come to the conclusion that obedience to God is a luxury that they can dispense with, at least until close to the end of their lives.

Those who practice the obedience of faith look for the future reward and set the greatest store by it. To their faith alone, the profit is exceedingly great. For them to take up the cross will be to carry a burden, but it will also be to find rest. They know the saying, "No cross, no crown." They recognize the truth that, if there is no obedience here on earth, there will be no future reward. This requires a faith that has eyes that can *"see afar off"* (2 Pet. 1:9), across the black torrent of death and within the veil that separates us from the unseen. A person will not obey God unless he has learned to endure *"as seeing him who is invisible"* (Heb. 11:27).

Unquestioning Obedience

Also, remember that the obedience that comes from true faith is often required to be altogether unhesitating and unquestioning, for it is written, *"He went out, not knowing whither he went."* God commanded Abraham to journey, and he moved his camp at once. Into the unknown land he made his way; through fertile regions or across a wilderness, among friends or through the midst of foes, he pursued his journey. He did not know where his way would take him, but he knew that the Lord had commanded him to go. Even bad men will obey God when they agree with Him, but good men will obey His commands even when they do not know what to think of them. It is not ours to judge the Lord's commands, but to follow them. I am weary of hearing people say, "Yes, we know that such a course would be right, but then the consequences might be painful: good men would be grieved, the cause would be weakened, and we ourselves would get into a world of trouble and put our hands into a hornet's nest." There is not much need to preach caution nowadays. Those who are willing to run any risk for the truth's sake are few enough. In the last few years, not many people have developed consciences that are tender about the Lord's honor. Prudent consideration of consequences is superabundant, but the spirit that obeys and dares all things for Christ's sake—where is it?

The Obedience of Faith

The Abrahams of today will not go out from the people and surroundings with which they are familiar. They will put up with anything sooner than risk their livelihoods. If they do go out, they must know where they are going and how much is to be gleaned in the new country. I am not pronouncing any judgment on their conduct, I am merely pointing out the fact. Our Puritan forefathers had little regard for property or liberty when these stood in the way of conscience; they defied exile and danger sooner than give up a grain of truth. But their descendants prefer peace and worldly amusements, and they pride themselves on "culture" rather than on heroic faith. The modern believer must have no mysteries. He must have everything planed down to a scientific standard. Abraham *went out, not knowing whither he went,* but people today must have every bit of information with regard to the way, and then they will not go. If they obey at all, it is because their own superior judgments tend in that direction. But, to go forth, not knowing where they are going, and to go at all hazards, is not to their liking at all. They are so highly "cultured" that they prefer to be original and to map out their own way.

My friend, having once discerned the voice of God, obey without question. If you have to

stand alone, and if nobody will befriend you,
stand alone, and God will befriend you. If you
should get an unfavorable word from those you
value most, bear it. What, after all, are unfavorable words or good words, compared with
keeping a clear conscience by walking in the
way of the Lord? The line of truth is as narrow
as a razor's edge, and the one who wants to
keep to such a line needs to wear the golden
sandals of the peace of God. Through divine
grace may we, like Abraham, walk with our
hand in the hand of the Lord, even where we
cannot see our way!

Continuous Obedience

The obedience that faith produces also
must be continuous. Having begun the separated life, Abraham continued to dwell in
tents, and to sojourn in the land that was far
from the place of his birth. His whole life may
be summed up in this way: *"By faith Abraham...obeyed."* He believed, and therefore he
walked before the Lord in a perfect way. He
even offered up his son Isaac. "Abraham's mis-
take," was it? How dare anyone talk in that
way! By faith he obeyed, and to the end of his
life he was never an original speculator or in-
ventor of ways for self-will, but a submissive

servant of that great Lord who condescended to call him *"Friend"* (James 2:23). May it be said of you that by faith you obeyed! Do not cultivate doubt, or you will soon cultivate disobedience. Set this up as your standard, and from now on let this be the epitome of your life: "By faith he obeyed."

The Life of Faith and Obedience

We must, therefore, wholeheartedly believe in God and eagerly serve Him. Now, what sort of life will result from our faith and obedience?

Life without Risk

We will live our lives without that great risk that otherwise holds us in peril. A person runs a great risk when he steers himself. Rocks or no rocks, the peril lies in the helmsman. However, the believer is no longer the helmsman of his own vessel; he has taken a Pilot on board. To believe in God and do what He commands is a great escape from the hazards of personal weakness and folly. If we do as God commands, and do not seem to succeed, it is no fault of ours. Failure itself would be success as long as we did not fail to obey.

If we were to pass through life unrecognized, or were only acknowledged by a sneer from the worldly-wise, and if this were regarded as a failure, it could be borne with calm confidence as long as we knew that we had kept our faith toward God and our obedience to Him. Providence is God's business; obedience is ours. What comes out of our life's course must remain with the Lord. To obey is our sole concern. What harvest will come from our sowing we must leave with the Lord of the harvest, but we ourselves must take care of the basket and the seed and scatter our handfuls in the furrows without fail. We can win, *"Well done, good and faithful servant"* (Matt. 25:23). To be a successful servant is not in our power, and we will not be held responsible for it. Our greatest risk is over when we obey. God makes faith and obedience the way of safety.

Life Free from the Heaviest Cares

Next, we will enjoy a life free from life's heaviest cares. If we were in the middle of Africa with Stanley, the newsman who found missionary Dr. David Livingstone, our pressing concern would be to find our way out. Yet, when we have nothing to do but to obey, our road is mapped out for us. Jesus says, *"Follow me"* (Matt. 4:19), and this makes our way plain and lifts a load of cares from our shoulders.

To choose our course by human reasoning is a way of thorns. To obey is like traveling on the king's highway. When we follow our own methods, we have to sail against the wind and try to get back to our original course, and we often miss the port after all. But faith, like a steamship, steers straight for the harbor's mouth and leaves a bright track of obedience behind her as she forges ahead.

When our only concern is to obey, a thousand other cares take flight. If we sin in order to succeed, we have sown the seeds of care and sorrow, and the reaping will be a grievous one. If we forsake the path and try shortcuts, we will have to do a degree of wading through mire and slough, we will spatter ourselves from head to foot, and we will be wearied trying to find our way—all because we could not trust God and obey His instructions. Obedience may appear difficult, and it may bring sacrifice with it, but, after all, it is the nearest and the best road. The ways of obedience are, in the long run, *"ways of pleasantness, and all her paths are peace"* (Prov. 3:17). The person who is always believing and obedient, through the strength of the Holy Spirit, has chosen the *"good part"* (Luke 10:42). It is he who can sing,

> I have no cares, O blessed Lord,
>> For all my cares are thine;
> I live in triumph, too, for thou
>> Hast made thy triumphs mine.

Or, to change the verse, he is like the shepherd boy in the Valley of Humiliation, from John Bunyan's *The Pilgrim's Progress,* for that lowland is part of the great Plain of Obedience, and he also can sing,

> He that is down need fear no fall,
>   He that is low no pride;
> He that is humble ever shall
>   Have God to be his Guide.

Although he may not reach the heights of ambition or stand on the dizzying cliffs of presumption, he will know superior joys. He has hit upon the happiest mode of living under heaven—a mode of life corresponding to the perfect life above. He will dwell in God's house and will be continually praising Him.

Life of the Highest Honor

Moreover, the way of obedience is a life of the highest honor. Obedience is the glory of a human life—the glory that our Lord Jesus has given to His chosen, even His own glory. *"Though he were a Son, yet learned he obedience by the things which he suffered"* (Heb. 5:8). He never forged an original course, but He always did the things that pleased the Father. Let this be our glory. By faith we yield our intelligence to the highest intelligence; we are led, guided, and directed, and we follow where our Lord has gone. To us who believe, He is honor. To a soldier it is the greatest honor to have accomplished his sovereign's command. He does not debase his manhood when he subjects it to honorable command. On the contrary, he is even exalted by obeying in the day of danger. It is no dishonor to have it said of us, as Tennyson did of the British cavalry in "The Charge of the Light Brigade,"

> Theirs not to reason why,
> Theirs but to do and die.

The bravest and the most honored of men are those who implicitly obey the command of the King of Kings. The best among His children are those who know their Father's mind the best and who yield to it the most joyful obedience. Within the walls of our Father's house, should we have any other ambition than to be perfectly obedient children before Him and implicitly trusting toward Him?

A Life of Communion with God

Yet, my friend, this is a kind of life that will bring communion with God. God often hides His face behind the clouds of dust that His children make by their self-will. If we transgress against Him, we will soon be in trouble. However, a holy walk—the walk described by our Scripture text as faith that produces obedience—is heaven beneath the stars. God comes down to walk with men who obey. If they walk with Him, He walks with them. The Lord can only have fellowship with His servants as they obey. Obedience is heaven in us, and it is the prelude to our being in heaven. Obedient faith is the way to eternal life; no, it is eternal life revealing itself.

A Life to Imitate

The obedience of faith creates a form of life that may be safely copied. As parents, we wish to live in such a way that our children may imitate us to their lasting profit. Teachers should aspire to be what they want their classes to be. If you have received your own schooling in the obedience of faith, you will be a good teacher. Children usually exaggerate their models, but there is no need to fear that they will go too far in faith or in obedience to the Lord. I like to hear a man say, when his father has gone, "My dear father was a man who feared God, and I desire to follow in his footsteps. When I was a boy, I thought he was rather stiff and puritanical, but now I see that he had a good reason for it all. I feel much the same myself, and would do nothing of which God would not approve."

The bringing up of families is a very important matter. This topic is neglected too much nowadays. However, it is the most profitable of all holy service and is the hope of the future. Great men, in the best sense, are bred in holy households. A God-fearing example at home is the most fruitful of religious agencies.

I knew a humble little church that belonged to one of the strictest sects of Christianity. There was nothing cultural about the ministry, but the people were staunch believers. Five or six families who attended that despised ministry learned to truly believe what they believed and to live it out. It was by no means a liberal creed that they received, but what they believed affected their lives. They became substantial in wealth and generous and benevolent in giving.

These families all sprang from plain, humble men who knew their Bibles and believed the doctrines of grace. They learned to fear God, to trust in Him, and to rest in the old faith; and they prospered even in worldly things. Their third generation descendants do not all adhere to their way of thinking, but they have risen through God's blessing on their grandfathers. These men were fed on substantial meat, and they became sturdy old fellows, able to cope with the world and to fight their way. I wish that we had more men today who would maintain truth at all costs. May the Lord give us back those whose examples can be safely copied in all things, even though they may be denounced as being "rigid" or "too precise." We serve a jealous God and a holy Savior. Let us make sure that we do not grieve His Spirit and cause Him to withdraw from us.

A Life That Needs Great Grace

In addition, faith that produces obedience is a kind of life that needs great grace. Those who profess faith but who are not diligent in practicing it will not live in this way. Maintaining the faith that obeys in everything requires watchfulness and prayer and nearness to God. Beloved, *"he giveth more grace"* (James 4:6). The Lord will enable you to add to your faith all the virtues (2 Pet. 1:5).

Whenever you fail in any respect in your life, do not sit down and question the goodness of God and the power of the Holy Spirit. That is not the way to increase the stream of obedience but to diminish the source of it. Believe more instead of less. Try, by God's grace, to believe more in the pardon of sin, more in the renovation by the Holy Spirit, more in the everlasting covenant, more in the love that had no beginning and will never, never cease. Your hope does not lie in rushing into the darkness of doubt but in returning repentantly into the still clearer light of a steadier faith. May you be helped to do so, and may we, and the whole multitude of the Lord's redeemed, by faith go on to obey our Lord in all things!

Remember, *"By faith Abraham...obeyed."* Have faith in God, and then obey, obey, obey, and keep on obeying, until the Lord calls you home. Obey on earth, and then you will have learned to obey in heaven. Obedience is the rehearsal of eternal bliss. Practice now, by obedience, the song that you will sing forever in glory. God grant His grace to us!

Chapter 2

"At Thy Word"

And Simon answering said unto him, Master,
we have toiled all the night, and have taken
nothing: nevertheless at thy word
I will let down the net.
—Luke 5:5

How very much may simple obedience involve the sublime! Peter went to catch up the net and let it down into the sea, and he said as naturally as can be, *"At thy word I will let down the net."* But even though his words were simple, he was there and then appealing to one of the greatest principles that rules among intelligent beings, and to the strongest force that sways the universe: *At thy word.*

Great God, it is at Your word that seraphim fly and cherubim bow! Your angels, which excel in strength, do Your commandments, attending to the voice of Your word (Ps. 103:20). At Your word, space and time first came into being, as well as everything else that exists.

The Cause of Causes

"At thy word." This phrase is the cause of causes, the beginning of God's creation. *"By the word of the LORD were the heavens made"* (Ps. 33:6); and by that Word the present composition of this round world was settled as it now stands.

When the earth was formless and dark, Your voice, O Lord, was heard, saying, *"Let there be light"* (Gen. 1:3), and at Your word light leaped forth. At Your word day and night took up their places, and at Your word the waters were divided from the waters by the firmament of heaven. At Your word the dry land appeared, and the seas retired to their channels. At Your word the globe was mantled over with green, and vegetable life began. At Your word the sun and moon and stars appeared, *"for signs, and for seasons, and for days, and years"* (Gen. 1:14). At Your word the living creatures filled the sea and air and land, and man at last appeared. We are well assured of all this, for by faith we know *"that the worlds were framed by the word of God"* (Heb. 11:3). When we act in conformity with the word of our Lord, we feel that we are in line with all the forces of the universe, traveling on the main track of all real existence. Would you not agree that this is a sublime condition, even though it is seen in the common deeds of our everyday life?

By the Word of His Power

It is not in creation alone that the word of the Lord is supreme. Its majestic power is also manifested in God's continual care toward the world. For the Lord upholds *"all things by the word of his power"* (Heb. 1:3). The Psalms are full of illustrations of this. His word runs very swiftly (Ps. 147:15). Snow and vapor and stormy wind are all fulfilling His word (Ps. 148:8). When the lakes and rivers are frozen over from the winter cold, the Lord sends forth His word and melts them (Ps. 147:16–18). We see that nature abides and moves by the word of the Lord.

So, too, all matters of fact and history are subject to the supreme Word. Jehovah stands as the center of all things. As Lord of all, He remains at the saluting point, and all the events of the ages come marching by at His word, bowing to His sovereign will. At Your word, O God, kingdoms arise and empires flourish. At Your word races of men become dominant and tread down their fellowmen. At Your word dynasties die, kingdoms crumble, mighty cities become deserts, and armies of men melt away like the frost of the morning. Despite the sin of man and the rage of devils, there is a sublime sense in which all things from the beginning, since Adam crossed the threshold of Eden even until now, have happened according to the purpose and will of the Lord of Hosts. Prophecy utters her oracles, and history writes her pages, at Your word, O Lord.

It is wonderful to think of the fisherman of Galilee letting down his net in perfect consonance with all the arrangements of the ages. Imagine the scene as Peter's net obeys the law that regulates the spheres. His hand consciously does what the star Arcturus and the constellation Orion are doing without thought. This little bell on the Galilean lake rings out in harmony with the everlasting chimes. *"At thy word,"* says Peter as he promptly obeys, therein repeating the watchword of seas and stars, of winds and worlds. It is glorious to be keeping step in this way with the marching of the armies of the King of Kings.

The Password of the Ages

There is another way of applying this concept. *"At thy word"* has been the password of all good men from the beginning until now. Saints have acted on these three words and found their marching orders in them. Go back in your imagination to the time of Noah. Imagine that an ark is being built on dry land, and that a ribald crowd has gathered about the old patriarch, and is laughing at him. Noah is not ashamed, for, lifting his face to heaven, he says, "I have built this great vessel, O Jehovah, at Your word."

Or think of Abraham as he abandons the place of his childhood, leaves his family, and goes with Sarah to a land of which he knows nothing. He crosses the broad Euphrates river and enters into a country possessed by the Canaanites, in which he will roam as a stranger and a sojourner all his days. He dwells in tents, as will Isaac and Jacob. If any scoff at him for thus renouncing the comforts of a settled life, he also lifts his calm face to heaven and smilingly answers to the Lord, "It is at Your word." Yes, and even when his brow is furrowed, and the hot tear is ready to force itself from beneath the Partriarch's eyelid as he lifts his hand with the knife to stab Isaac to the heart, if any charge him with murder, or think that he is mad, he lifts the same calm face toward the majesty of the Most High and says, "It is at Your word." At that word, he joyfully sheathes the sacrificial knife, for he has proven his willingness to go to the utmost at the word of the Lord his God.

If I were to introduce you to a thousand of the faithful ones who have shown the obedience of faith, in every case they would justify their acts by telling you that they did them at God's word. Imagine Moses lifting his rod in the presence of the haughty Pharaoh. He does not lift that rod in vain at Jehovah's word, for the plagues fall thick and heavy upon the Egyptians. They are made to know that God's word does not return to Him void, but accomplishes His purpose (Isa. 55:11), whether it is a threat or a promise.

Then, see Moses lead the people out of Egypt, the whole host with its multitudes! Notice how he brings them to the Red Sea, where the wilderness shuts them in. The heights frown on either side, and the rattle of Egypt's war chariots is behind them. How did Moses come to play the fool and bring them here? Were there no graves in Egypt that he therefore brought them out to die on the Red Sea shore? Moses' answer is the quiet reflection that he did it at Jehovah's word. And we see that God justifies that word, for the sea opens wide a highway for the elect of God, and they march joyfully through. On the other side, with tambourines and dances they sing to the Lord who has triumphed gloriously.

Now, imagine Joshua surrounding and attacking Jericho. He does not use battering rams. He only uses one great blast of trumpets. His reason for doing so is that God has spoken to him by His word. And so, let us move directly on, for time would fail me to speak of Samson and Jephthah and Barak (Heb. 11:32): these men did what they did at God's word, and, as they did so, the Lord was with them.

The Sublimity of Simple Obedience

Is it bringing things down from the sublime to the ridiculous to talk of Peter and the net that he cast over the side of his little boat? Not at all. We are ourselves ridiculous when we do not make our own lives sublime by the obedience of faith. Certainly, there may be as much sublimity in casting a net as in building an ark, lifting a rod, or sounding a ram's horn; and it is clear that, if it is done in faith, the simplest action of life may be sublimely great. The crash of the wave as it covered Peter's net may have been as sublime before the Lord as was the thunderous glory of the Red Sea when the waters returned in their strength. God, who sees the world as *"a drop of a bucket"* (Isa. 40:15), sees wonders in the smallest act of faith.

Do not, I implore you, think that sublimity lies in great quantities, to be measured by a scale, so that a mile is considered sublime and an inch is considered absurd. We do not measure what is moral and spiritual by rods and chains. The common act of fishing at Christ's word links Peter with all the principalities and powers and forces that, in all ages, have known this as their only law: *"He spake, and it was done; he commanded, and it stood fast"* (Ps. 33:9). We, too, will have fellowship with the sublime if we know how to be perfectly obedient to the Word of the Lord.

The Rule of All Christians

"At thy word" ought to be the rule of all Christians for all aspects of their lives. This rule should direct us in the church and in the world; it should guide us in our spiritual beliefs and in our secular acts. I wish it were so. We hear boasting that the Bible, and the Bible alone, is the religion of Protestants. It is a mere boast. Few Protestants can honestly repeat the assertion. They have other books to which they pay deference, and other rules and other guides beyond, above, and even in opposition to, the one Word of God. It ought not to be so. The power of the church and the power

of the individual to please God will never be fully known until we get back to the simple yet sublime rule of our text: *"At thy word."*

This rule has many applications, and I am just going to hammer on this phrase as God helps me. To begin, I will somewhat repeat myself by explaining that it ought to apply to the affairs of ordinary life. Next, I will show you how it should also apply to matters of spiritual profit. And then I will illustrate how it ought to find its chief application in our great life business, which is being *"fishers of men"* (Matt. 4:19).

In the Affairs of Ordinary Life

"At thy word" should apply to all aspects of ordinary life. For example, we should obey God's Word in regard to continuing in honest industry. *"Let every man abide in the same calling wherein he was called"* (1 Cor. 7:20). Many people in the present trying financial crisis are half ready to resign from their work, or run away from their businesses, because they have toiled all night and have nothing to show for it. It is true that the financial darkness has lasted a long time and does not yet yield to the dawning. But, still, Christians must not murmur or leave their posts. Even

though you are being tried, continue to be diligent in your business, and still *"provide things honest in the sight of all men"* (Rom. 12:17). Labor on in hope. Say just as Peter did, *"Nevertheless at thy word I will let down the net."*

"Except the LORD build the house, they labour in vain that build it" (Ps. 127:1). You know that truth very well. Know this also, that the Lord will not forsake His people. Your best endeavors will not, of themselves, bring you prosperity. Still, do not relax those endeavors. Since God's Word tells you to conduct yourselves like men and to *"be strong"* (1 Cor. 16:13), then *"gird up the loins of your mind*[s], *be sober"* (1 Pet. 1:13), and *"stand fast"* (1 Cor. 16:13). Do not throw away your shields (see Ephesians 6:16); do not cast away your confidence (Heb. 10:35), but stand steadily in your rank until the tide of battle turns. God has placed you where you are. Do not move until His providence calls you. Do not run in the presence of the dark cloud. Open your doors tomorrow morning, display your goods, and do not let despondency drive you to anything that is rash or unseemly. Say, *"Nevertheless at thy word I will let down the net."*

If I am speaking to any who are out of work just now, searching for some place where they can provide bread for themselves and for their families, as is their duty, let them hear and consider this. If any man does not do his best to provide for his own household, he does not come under a gospel blessing, but he is said to be worse than a heathen and a publican (1 Tim. 5:8). It is the duty of us all to work at something honorable, so that we may have enough to give to the needy as well as to those dependent on us.

If, after having gone about the city until your feet are blistered, you can find nothing to do, do not sit at home next Monday, sulkily saying, "I will not try again." Apply our Scripture text to this painful trial, and yet again venture out in hope, saying with Peter, *"We have toiled all the night, and have taken nothing: nevertheless at thy word I will let down the net."* Let people see that a Christian is not readily driven to despair. No, let them see that when the yoke is made more heavy, the Lord has a secret way of strengthening the backs of His children to bear their burdens.

If the Holy Spirit makes you calmly resolute, you will honor God much more by your happy perseverance than will the talkative by his fine speeches or the formalist by his outward show. Common life is the true place in which to prove the truth of godliness and bring glory to God. Not by doing extraordinary works, but by the piety of ordinary life, is the Christian known and his faith honored. At God's Word hold on, even to the end. *"Trust in the LORD, and do good; so shalt thou dwell in the land, and verily thou shalt be fed"* (Ps. 37:3).

It may be, too, that you have been endeavoring in your daily life to acquire skill in your business, and have not succeeded, or that you have tried to acquire more knowledge, so that you could better fulfill your vocation, but up to this time you have not prospered as you could wish to. Do not, therefore, cease from your efforts. Christians must never be idlers. Our Lord Jesus would never have it said that His disciples are the sort of cowards who, if they do not succeed the first time, will never try again. We are to be patterns of all the moral virtues as well as the spiritual graces. Therefore, as the Lord commands, work on with mind and hand, and look to Him for the blessing. At His word, let down the net once more. He may intend to bless you abundantly, when by trial you have been prepared to bear the blessing.

This truth will apply very closely to those who are working hard to train children. It may be that with your own children you have not yet succeeded: the boy's spirit may still be wild

and proud, and the girl may not yet have
yielded to obedience and submission. Or, you
may be working in the Sunday school or in an
elementary school, trying to impart knowledge
and to mold the youthful mind to what is right,
and you may have been baffled. But, if it is
your business to teach, do not be overcome.
Stand firm at your work as though you heard
Jesus say, *"Whatsoever ye do, do it heartily, as
to the Lord, and not unto men"* (Col. 3:23).
Earnestly, then, at His word, again let down
the net.

I counsel you, dear friends, in everything
to which you set your hands, if it is a good
thing, do it with all your might; and if it is not
a good thing, have nothing to do with it. It is
possible that you are called to teach this generation some moral truth. In most generations
individuals have been called to carry out re-
forms and to promote progress. You are bound
to *"love thy neighbour as thyself"* (Matt. 22:39);
therefore, as you have opportunity, *"do good
unto all men"* (Gal. 6:10). If you have tried
and, up to this point, have not won a hearing,
do not give up your position. If it is a good
thing, and you are a Christian, never let it be
said that you are afraid or ashamed. I admire
in Palissy the potter, not only his Christianity,
which could not be overcome by persecution,

but his perseverance in his own business of making pottery. His last farthing and his last breath would have gone to discovering a glaze or bringing out a color. I love to see such people believers. I would not like to see our Lord followed by a set of cowards who could not fight the common battles of life. How could such weaklings become worthy of the lordlier chivalry that wrestles with *"spiritual wickedness in high places"* (Eph. 6:12)? It is for us to be the bravest among the brave in the plains of common life, so that when we are summoned to higher fields, where still greater deeds are needed, we may go there trained for the higher service.

Does it seem to you that it is a little out of place for me, a pastor, to be talking in this way? I do not think so. I notice that in the Old Testament we are told about the sheep and the cattle and the fields and the harvests of good men, and that all of these things had to do with their faith. I notice how the prudent woman, according to Solomon, looked well to her household. (See Proverbs 31:10–31.) And I observe that in the Bible we have the books of Proverbs and Ecclesiastes; there is little spiritual teaching in either of them, but they contain a great deal of good, sound, practical common sense. It is evident to me that the

Lord does not intend our faith to be penned up in a pew, but to be lived out in our places of business, and to be seen in every realm of life.

The great principle of our Scripture text came from the lips of a workingman, and to the workingman I return it. It was connected with a net and a boat, the implements of his labor, and with these common things I would link it. And I would say to all who serve the Lord in this present evil world: In the name of God, if you have anything to do, do not be so despondent and despairing as to cease from it, but, according to His word, once more go forward in your honest endeavors and, like Peter, say, *"I will let down the net."* This may prove to be a word in season to some who are weary of the hardness of the times. I will rejoice if it strengthens an arm or cheers a heart. Have faith in God, my tried friends. *"Be ye stedfast, unmoveable, always abounding in the work of the Lord"* (1 Cor. 15:58).

In Matters of Spiritual Growth

In matters of salvation and spiritual growth, we must, at the word of Christ, let down the net again. I put this, first, to those of you who have gone to church a great many times—with sincerity, if you are to be believed—hoping to find salvation. You have prayed before the sermon began that the Lord would really bless the sermon to you. Now, I want you to consider my words carefully: I do not understand you at all; I cannot comprehend you, because the way of salvation is open to you at this very moment, and it is, *"Believe on the Lord Jesus Christ, and thou shalt be saved"* (Acts 16:31). You have nothing to wait for, and all your waiting is sinful.

If you say you are waiting for the stirring of the pool (see John 5:2–4), I tell you that there is no pool to be stirred and no angel to stir it. That pool was dried up long ago, and angels never go that way now. Our Lord Jesus Christ closed up the Bethesda pool when He came and said to the man lying there, *"Rise, take up thy bed, and walk"* (John 5:8). That is what He says to you. You have no business waiting. However, if you are waiting, I earnestly invite you to believe and live. Let down the net once more, and let it down this way: say, *"Lord, I believe; help thou mine unbelief"* (Mark 9:24). Breathe a prayer now to Jesus that He would accept you. Submit yourself to Him and implore Him to become—now, at this moment—your Savior. You will be heard. Plenty of fish are waiting to be taken in the net of faith. At the Lord's word, let it down.

But I will now speak to others who have been letting down their nets, in vain, perhaps, in the form of persistent prayer. Have you been praying for the conversion of a relative or pleading for some other good thing that you believe is according to the will of God, and after long pleading—pleading during the night, for your spirit has been sad—are you tempted never to offer that petition anymore? Now then, at Christ's word, who said, *"Men ought always to pray, and not to faint"* (Luke 18:1), and at the inspired Word of God, which says, *"Pray without ceasing"* (1 Thess. 5:17), let down the net, and pray again. Pray, not because the circumstances that surround you are more favorable, but simply because God commands you to *"continue in prayer"* (Col. 4:2). And, who knows? This very time you may meet with success!

Or, have you been searching the Scriptures to find a promise that will suit your situation? Do you want to get hold of some good word from God that will comfort you? Schools of such fish are around your boat; the sea of Scripture is full of them—fish of promise, I mean. But, the sad thing is that you have not been able to catch one of them. Nevertheless, try again. Search the Scriptures again with prayer, and implore the Holy Spirit to apply a precious portion to your heart, so that you may by faith enjoy the sweetness of it.

Perhaps you will obtain your desire this very day and receive a larger blessing than your mind can fully contain, so that in your case also the net will break from the fullness of the favor.

Or, it may be that you have been seeking some holy attainment for a long while. You want to conquer a persistent sin, exercise firmer faith, exhibit more zeal, and be more useful, but you have not yet gained your desire. Now then, since it is the Lord's desire that you should be *"perfect in every good work to do his will"* (Heb. 13:21), do not cease from your purpose, but at His word let down your net again. Never despair. That temper of yours will be conquered yet; that unbelief of yours will give way to holy faith. Let down the net, and all the graces may yet be taken in it, to be yours for the rest of your life. At Christ's word alone, still labor for the best things, and He will give them to you.

Or, are you seeking right now the closer presence of Christ and a nearer fellowship with Him? Are you yearning for a sight of His face, that face that outshines the morning? Do you wish to be brought into His banqueting house to be filled with His love? And have you cried in vain? Then cry once more, *"At thy word,"* for He asks you to come to Him. His loving voice invites you to draw near. At His word press forward once again, let down the net once more, and unspeakable joys await you, surpassing all you have experienced up to now.

So you see that the great principle of our text may justly be applied to our spiritual growth and benefit. God help us by His gracious Spirit to carry it out from day to day.

In the Lifework of Every Christian

This great principle should also be applied to our lifework. And what is the lifework of every Christian? Is it not soulwinning? To glorify God by bringing others to faith in Christ is the great purpose for which we still remain here on earth; otherwise, we would have been caught up to swell the harmony of the heavenly songs. It is expedient for many wandering sheep here below that we should remain here until we have brought them home to the great Shepherd and Bishop of their souls (1 Pet. 2:25).

Our way of winning men for Christ—or, to use His own metaphor, our method of catching men (Luke 5:10)—is by letting down the net of the Gospel. We have learned no other way of "holy fishing." Men with great zeal and little knowledge are inventing ingenious methods for catching men. However, for my part, I believe in nothing but letting down the gospel net by proclaiming the story of God's love toward men in Christ Jesus.

No new Gospel has been committed to us by Jesus, and He has authorized no new way of making it known. Our Lord has called all of us to the work of proclaiming free pardon through His blood to all who believe in Him. Each believer is authorized by Christ to seek the conversion of his friends and associates. May not every person seek to save his brother from the burning? Must not Jesus smile on anyone's endeavor to deliver his neighbor from going down to eternal death? Has He not said, *"Let him that heareth say, Come"* (Rev. 22:17)?

Whoever hears the Gospel is to invite others to come to Christ. The Word of the Lord is our authorization for keeping to our one work of making known the Gospel. It would be a sorry act of mutiny if we were either to be silent or to preach *"another gospel"* (2 Cor. 11:4), which would not be any gospel at all. The Word of the Lord is a warrant that justifies the man who obeys it. *"Where the word of a king is, there is power"* (Eccl. 8:4). What higher authority can we need?

The Results Are God's Responsibility

"Oh, but," some say, "you ought to advance to something higher than the mere elementary doctrine of grace and give the people something more in keeping with the progress of the times." We will not do so while Jesus commands us to go *"into all the world, and preach the gospel to every creature"* (Mark 16:15). If we do what He commands us, the responsibility of the matter no longer rests with us. Whatever comes of it, we are clear if we have obeyed orders. A servant is not to justify his master's message, but to deliver it. This makes it a joy to preach, this doing it at His word. Our business is to do what Christ tells us, as Christ tells us, and to do this again and again, as long as we have breath in our bodies. The commanding word continually cries to us, "Preach the Gospel, preach the Gospel to every creature!" Our justification for setting forth *"Christ crucified"* (1 Cor. 1:23), and incessantly inviting men to believe and live, lies in the same word that commanded Peter to walk on the sea and Moses to draw water out of a rock.

The result of this preaching will justify Christ who commanded it. No man, in the end, will be able to say to the Savior, "You set before your servants an impossible task, and You gave them an instrument to wield that was not at all adapted to produce its purpose." Instead, at the culmination of all things, it will be seen that for the salvation of the elect there was no better

way of redemption than a crucified Savior. It
will also be seen that there was no better means
to make the crucified Savior known than by the
simple proclamation of His Word by honest lips
in the power of the Spirit of the Lord. The fool-
ishness of preaching will turn out to be the
great proof of the wisdom of God.

My friends, you who teach or preach from
the pulpit or distribute tracts or speak personally to individuals—you do not need to be
afraid. Wisdom will exonerate herself from all
charges and vindicate her own methods. You
may be called a fool today for preaching the
Gospel, but that accusation, like rust on a
sword, will wear off as you use the weapon in
the wars of the Lord. The preaching of the
Word soon puts down all outcries against itself;
those protests mainly arise because the Word
is not preached. No one calls the Gospel weak
where it is smiting right and left like a great
two-handed sword. Our reply to the outcry
about the failure of the pulpit is to get into it
and preach the Gospel *"with the Holy Ghost
sent down from heaven"* (1 Pet. 1:12).

Obedience Is Our Responsibility

Indeed, this word of Christ, whereby He
gives us His authorization for letting down the

net, is such that it amounts to a command, and we will be found guilty if we do not obey. Suppose Simon Peter had said, "We have toiled all night and have taken nothing. Therefore, despite Your word, I will not let down the net"? Then Simon Peter would have been guilty of disobedience to his Lord and blasphemy against the Son of God.

What can I say to my fellow Christians who profess to be called of God, to be Christ's disciples, and yet never let down the net? Is it true that you are doing nothing for the truth, that you never disseminate the Gospel? Is it true that you call yourselves lights of the world and yet never shine, that you are sowers of the seed and yet forget that you have a seed basket? Am I addressing anyone who is wasting his life in this respect? Is it true that it is professedly your life's purpose to be a fisher of men and yet you have never cast a net or even helped to draw one on shore? Are you living under false pretenses? Are you mocking God by a fruitless profession that you never try to make fruitful? I do not have the strength with which to condemn you, but I pray to God that your own conscience might fulfill that service.

What can be said of the person who has been given a charge by the Lord to make known the glad tidings of salvation from eternal misery and yet is sinfully silent? The Great Physician has entrusted you with the medicine that heals the sick. You see them die around you, but you never speak of the remedy! The great King has given you the meal with which to feed the hungry, and you lock the storehouse door while the crowds are starving in your streets. This is a crime that may well make a man of God weep over you.

For example, the great city of London is growing ungodly to the very core, and yet our Lord has given the Gospel into the hands of His churches. What can be the reason for the indifference of the godly? If we keep this Gospel to ourselves, certainly coming ages will harshly condemn us as cruel to our posterity. Succeeding generations will point to our era and say, "What sort of people were these, who had the light but shut it up in a dark lantern?" In a century to come, when others will stand in our cities and walk in our streets, they will say, "A curse upon the memory of the ministers and people who failed in their duty, who came to the kingdom in a solemn time but never realized their calling, and who therefore missed the end and purpose of their being!" May we be spared from such a calamity as this. Yes, we have the authorization for working to spread the truth of God; and more than that, we have a statute from the throne, a peremptory command, and it will be to our grief if we do not preach the Gospel.

An All-Powerful Authorization

Now, my friends, this authorization from Christ is one which, if we are in the state of heart that Simon Peter was, will be omnipotent with us. It was very powerful with Simon Peter. For, observe, he was under the influence of a great disappointment—*"we have toiled all the night"* —yet he let down the net. Some say, "We have had all this gospel preaching, we have had all these revivals, all these stirrings, and nothing has come of it." When was that? I hear a good deal of this talk, but what are the facts? "Oh," they say, "you know we had a great deal of revival a little while ago." I do not know anything of the sort. We have had flashes of light here and there, but they have been comparatively so little that it is a pity to make so much of them. Moreover, considering the little that has ever been done for it, the spread of the Gospel has been marvelous.

Look at the current gospel work in India! People say that the Christian faith is not spreading. I say that it is spreading wonderfully compared with the labor that has been expended and the sacrifice that has been made. If in that land you spend a penny and get a thousand English pounds, you have no right to say, "What is that? We want a million." If your desires are that exacting, prove their sincerity by corresponding action. Increase your outlay. The harvest is wonderful considering the little amount of seed that has been sown, but if you wish for more sheaves, sow more. The church has had an enormous return for what little she has done.

In England there have been partial revivals, but to what have they amounted? A flash of light has been seen in a certain district, but darkness has still remained supreme over the length and breadth of the country. The newspapers have reported a great work in a certain spot, but if the papers had reported the places in which there has been no revival, we would have a different view of things! A little corner at the top of a column would have sufficed for the good, and column after column would not have sufficed to make known the black side of the situation.

The fact is that the church has scarcely ever been in a state of universal revival since the Day of Pentecost. There has been a partial moving among Christians every now and then, but the whole body throughout has never burned and flamed with the earnestness that the grand cause demands. Oh, that the Lord would set the whole church on fire! We have no cause whatsoever for disappointment. In proportion to the little effort expended, great things have come to us. Therefore, let us get to our nets again, and say no more about the night in which we have toiled.

Don't Lose Heart

Next, this command overcame Peter's love of ease. Evidently he was tired when he said, *"We have toiled all the night."* Fishing is hard work, especially when no fish are caught. It is natural to wish to be excused from further toil when you are already weary with unrewarded labor. I have heard some Christians say, "You know I had my time in the Sunday school years ago, and I used to wear myself out." No doubt their efforts were stupendous in the remote ages of their youthful zeal; we can hardly imagine what they must have been like, for no relic remains to assist our conceptions. At this time they feel authorized to take things easy, for they owe no more to their Lord, or at least they do not intend to pay any more.

Is it true that any one of us can cease from service when it is plain that we do not cease receiving mercy at the Lord's hands? Are we not ashamed of the situation when it is made clear to us? "Take it easy," people say. Yes, soon, very soon, we will take it easy, for there will be rest enough in the grave. Just now, while the souls of men are perishing, to relax our efforts is wickedness. No, Peter, although you now may be in a dripping sweat from having toiled all night, you must get at it again. He does so. The night's work is nothing; he must work in the day, too, if he is to catch fish.

No Command of Christ Is Out of Season

Moreover, the command of Christ was so supreme over Peter that he was not held back by carnal reason, for reason would say, "If you could not catch fish in the night, you will certainly not do so in the day." Night was the special time for taking fish on the Gennesaret lake; and by day, when the garish sun was lighting up the waves and letting the fish see every single mesh of the net, they were not likely to come into it. But when Christ commands, the most unlikely time is likely, and the most unpromising sphere becomes hopeful. No act is out of season when Christ commands it. If He says, "Go," go at once, without deliberation. Do not say, *"There are yet four months, and then cometh harvest"* (John 4:35). Jesus says that the fields *"are white already to harvest"* (v. 35). Peter lets down the net at once, and wisely does he act at Christ's word.

You Must Personally Let Down the Net

The lesson to you and to me is this: Let us do as Peter did, and let down the net *personally,* for the apostle said, *"I will let down the net."* Brother, can you not do something with your own heart, lips, and hands? Sister, can you not do something with your own gentle spirit? You may say, "I was thinking about getting half a dozen friends to form a committee to relieve the poor around us." Nothing will ever come of it; the poor will not get a bowl of soup or a hunk of bread. Go about it yourself. You may reply, "But I think I might get a dozen people to come together and organize a society." Yes, and then you would move resolutions and amendments all day long and finish up by passing votes of mutual commendation. You had better get to work yourself, as Peter did.

And you had better do it at once, for Peter immediately let down the net, as soon as he had launched out into the deep. You may never have another opportunity; your zeal may evaporate, or your life may end. Peter, however, only let down one net, and there was the pity of it. If John and James and all the rest had let down their nets, the result would have been much better. "Why?" you ask. Because, since there was only one net, that net was overstrained and it broke. If all the nets had been used, they might have taken more fish, and no net would have been broken.

I was reading some time ago of a catch of mackerel at Brighton, England. When the net was full, the mackerel sticking in all the meshes made it so heavy that the fishermen could not raise it, and the boat itself was in some danger of going down, so they had to cut away the net and lose the fish. If there had been many nets and boats, the fishermen might have buoyed up all of the fish, and so they might have done in this case in our text. As it was, many fish were lost through the breaking of the net.

If a church can be so awakened that each individual gets to work in the power of the Holy Spirit, and then all the individuals combine, how many souls will be captured for Jesus! Multitudes of souls are lost to the blessed Gospel because of our broken nets; the nets get broken because we are not truly united in holy service. By our lack of wisdom we bring about

loss to our Master's cause. Ministers would not
need to become worn out with work if everyone
would do his share; one boat would not begin
to sink if each of the other boats took a part of
the blessed load.

Now, my friends, if I have accomplished
anything by the help of God's Spirit, I hope I
have made you ready to accept the following
guidance for service, drawn from the text. The
way in which to serve God is to do it at His
word. I pray that none of us may sink into
serving the Lord as a matter of routine. May
we never fall into serving Him in our own
strength. We must preach, teach, and work in
His name because we hear Him calling us to do
so. We must act at His word. If this were the
case, we would work with much more faith,
with much more earnestness, and with much
more likelihood of success.

It is a blessed thing to see Christ sitting in
the boat while you cast out the net. If you
catch a glimpse of His approving smile as He
watches you, you will work very heartily. You
will stand there doing a thing that critics sneer
at as absurd, but you will do it in all confidence, believing that it must be wise, because
Jesus asks you to do it. We must labor in entire
dependence on Him, not preaching or teaching
because in our judgment it is the right thing to

do—Peter did not think so—but because Jesus gives the word, and His word is law. You may not work because you have any expectation of success from the excellence of your work or from the nature of the people among whom you labor, but because Jesus has given you the word.

I remember well how some of my brothers used to talk to me. They said, "You preach the Gospel to dead sinners; you ask them to repent and believe. You might just as well shake a handkerchief over a grave and command the corpse to come out of it." Exactly so. They spoke the truth, but then, I would delight to go and shake a handkerchief over graves and command the dead to live if Jesus called me to do so. I would expect to see the cemetery crack and heave from end to end if I were sent on such an errand by the Lord. I would accept the duty joyfully.

The more absurd the wise men of our age make the Gospel out to be and the more they show that it is powerless to produce the intended purpose, the more we will persevere in our old method of preaching Jesus crucified. Our resolves are not to be shaken by that mode of reasoning. We never have drawn our argument for preaching the Gospel from the work itself but from the orders given us to do it, and we would rather act on the responsibility of Christ than on our own.

I would rather be a fool and do what Christ tells me than be the wisest man of the modern school of thought and despise the Word of the Lord. I would rather lay the responsibility for my life at the feet of Him who commands me to live according to His Word than seek out a purpose in life for myself and feel that the responsibility rested on my own shoulders. Let us be willing to be under orders to Christ, willing to persevere under difficulties, willing to begin anew in His service from this very hour.

Chapter 3

Elijah's Plea

Let it be known this day...that I have done all
these things at thy word.
—1 Kings 18:36

The acts of Elijah were very singular. It had not been known from the foundations of the earth that a man would shut up the doors of rain for more than three years. Yet we read in 1 Kings that Elijah suddenly leaps on the scene, announces the judgment of the Lord, and then disappears for a time. When he reappears, at God's command, he orders Ahab to gather the priests of Baal and to put to the test the question of whether Baal or Jehovah was indeed God. Bullocks would be slain and laid upon the wood, without fire, and the God who would answer by fire would be determined to be the one living and true God, the God of Israel.

We might question within ourselves what right the prophet had to restrain the clouds or to put God's honor to a test. Suppose the Lord had not willed to answer Elijah by fire; did he have any right to make the glory of God hang upon such terms as he proposed? The answer is that he had done all these things according to God's word. It was no whim of his to chastise the nation with a drought. It was no scheme of his, concocted in his own brain, that he should put the divinity of Jehovah or of Baal to the test by a sacrifice to be consumed by miraculous fire. Oh, no! If you read through the life of Elijah, you will see that whenever he takes a step, it is preceded by, *"The word of the LORD came to Elijah."* (See 1 Kings 17–21.) He never acts by himself; God is behind him. He moves according to the divine will, and he speaks according to the divine teaching. He pleads this fact with the Most High, saying, *"Let it be known this day...that I have done all these things at thy word."*

This makes the character of Elijah stand out, not as an example of reckless daring, but as the example of a man of sound mind. Faith in God is true wisdom. Childlike confidence in the Word of God is the highest form of common sense. To believe Him who cannot lie and to trust in Him who cannot fail is a kind of wisdom that none but fools will laugh at. The wisest of men must concur with the opinion that it is always best to place your reliance where it will certainly be justified, and always best to believe what cannot possibly be false.

Imagine Elijah before the priests of Baal. He had believed God implicitly, and had acted on his belief, and now he naturally expects to be justified in what he has done. An ambassador never dreams that his authorized acts will be repudiated by his king. If a man acts as your agent and does as you direct, the responsibility for his actions lies with you, and you must back him up. It would, indeed, be an atrocious thing to send a servant on an errand and, when he had faithfully performed it to the letter, to deny sending him.

It is not so with God. If we will only trust Him enough to do as He commands, He will never fail us. He will see us through, though earth and hell should stand in the way. It may not be today or tomorrow, but as surely as the Lord lives, the time will come when he who trusted in Him will have joy as a result of His trustworthiness. Obedient believers can take Elijah's plea as a firm basis for prayer. And for those who cannot say that they have acted according to God's Word, it is a solemn matter to consider.

A Firm Basis for Prayer

Perhaps you are a minister of God or a worker in the cause of Christ, and you are going forth and preaching the Gospel with many tears and prayers and are continuing to use every means that Christ has ordained. Are you saying to yourself, "May I expect to have fruit out of all this?" Of course you may. You are not being sent on a frivolous errand. You are not called to sow dead seed that will never spring up. Therefore, when that anxiety weighs heavily on your heart, go to the mercy seat with this as one of your arguments: "Lord, I have acted according to Your Word. Now let it be seen that it is so. I have preached Your Word, and You have said, *'It shall not return unto me void'* (Isa. 55:11). I have prayed for these people, and You have said, *'The effectual fervent prayer of a righteous man availeth much'* (James 5:16); let it be seen that this is according to Your Word."

Perhaps you are a teacher. You can say, "I have brought my children in supplication before You, and I have gone forth, after studying Your Word, to teach them, to the best of my ability, the way of salvation. Now, Lord, I claim it of Your truth that You should justify my teaching and my expectation by allowing

me to see the souls of my children saved by
You, through Jesus Christ, Your Son." Do you
not see that you have a good argument, if the
Lord has appointed you to do this work? He
has, as it were, bound Himself by that very fact
to support you in the doing of it.

If you, with holy diligence and carefulness,
do all these things according to His Word, then
you may come with certainty to the throne of
grace and say to Him, "Do as You have said.
Have You not said, *'He that goeth forth and
weepeth, bearing precious seed, shall doubtless
come again with rejoicing, bringing his sheaves
with him'* (Ps. 126:6)? Lord, I have done that.
Give me my sheaves. You have said, *'Cast thy
bread upon the waters: for thou shalt find it
after many days'* (Eccl. 11:1). Lord, I have done
that, and therefore I implore You to fulfill
Your promise to me." You may plead in this
fashion with the same boldness that made Elijah say in the presence of all the people, *"Let it
be known this day that thou art God in Israel,
and that I am thy servant, and that I have done
all these things at thy word"* (1 Kings 18:36).

Next, I would apply this teaching to
churches. I am afraid that many churches are
not prospering. The congregations are thin,
the churches are diminishing, the prayer
meetings are scantily attended, and spiritual

life is low. If I can conceive of a church in such a condition, which, nevertheless, can say to God, "We have done all these things at Your Word," I would expect to see that church soon revived in answer to prayer.

The reason why some churches do not prosper is because they have not done according to God's Word. They have not even cared to know what God's Word says. Another book is their standard. Instead of the inspired Word of God, a man is their leader and legislator. Some churches are doing little or nothing for the conversion of sinners. But anyone, in any church, who can go before God and say, "Lord, we have had among us the preaching of the Gospel, and we have earnestly prayed for the blessing. We have gathered about your minister, and we have held him up in the arms of prayer and faith. We have, as individual Christians, sought out our particular realms of service, we have all gone out to bring in souls to You, and we have lived in godliness of life by the help of Your grace. Now, therefore, prosper Your cause," he will find it a good plea. Real prosperity must come to any church that walks according to Christ's rules, obeys Christ's teaching, and is filled with Christ's Spirit. I would exhort all members of churches that are in a poor way right now to see to it that all things are done according to God's Word and then to wait in hope in holy confidence. The fire from heaven must come. The blessing cannot be withheld.

The same principle also may be applied to any individual believers who are in trouble because they have done what is right. It often happens that a man feels, "I could make money, but I must not, for the proposed course of action would be wrong. Such a situation is open, but it involves that which my conscience does not approve. I will suffer instead of profiting by doing anything that is questionable." It may be that you are in great trouble, clearly through your obedience to God. In that case, you are the one above all others who may lay this case before the Most High: "Lord, I have done all these things at Your Word, and you have said, *'I will never leave thee, nor forsake thee'* (Heb. 13:5). I implore You to intervene for me." Somehow or other God will provide for you. If He intends for you to be tried further, He will give you strength to bear it. But it is likely that now that He has tested you, He will bring you forth from the fire as gold (Job 23:10).

> Do good and know no fear,
> For so thou in the land shalt dwell,
> And God thy food prepare.

In addition, I would like to apply this principle to the seeking sinner. You are anxious to be saved. You are attentive to the Word, and your heart says, "Let me know what this salvation is and how to approach it, for I will have it no matter what stands in the way." You have heard Jesus say, *"Strive to enter in at the strait gate"* (Luke 13:24). You have heard His appeal, *"Labour not for the meat which perisheth, but for that meat which endureth unto everlasting life"* (John 6:27). You long to enter the narrow gate and to eat of the meat that endures; you would give worlds for such a gift. You have spoken well, my friend. Now, listen. You cannot have heaven through your actions, as a matter of merit. There is no merit possible for you, for you have sinned and are already condemned. But God has laid down certain lines upon which He has promised to meet you and to bless you. Have you followed those lines? For, if you have, He will not be false to you.

It is written, *"He that believeth and is baptized shall be saved"* (Mark 16:16). Can you come before God and say, "I have believed and have been baptized"? Then you are on firm pleading ground. It is also written, *"whoso confesseth and forsaketh* [his sins] *shall have mercy"* (Prov. 28:13). When you have confessed your sins and forsaken them, you have a just claim upon the promise of God, and you can say to Him, "Lord, fulfill this word for Your servant, upon which You have caused me to hope. There is no merit in my faith, my baptism, my repentance, or my forsaking of sin. Yet, as You have put Your promise side by side with these things, and I have been obedient to You in regard to them, I now come to You and say, 'Prove Your own truth, for I have done all these things at Your word.'"

No sinner will come before God in the end and say, "I trusted as You asked me to trust, and yet I am lost." It is impossible. Your blood, if you are lost, will be on your own head. But you will never be able to lay your soul's damnation at the door of God. He is not false; it is you who are false.

You see, then, how the principle can be applied in prayer: "I have done these things at Your word; therefore, O Lord, do as You have said."

Have You Been Faithful to God's Word?

We will go over the same ground a little, while I ask you to put yourself through your paces—to examine yourself regarding whether or not you have done all these things at God's Word.

Let every Christian worker who has not been successful answer these questions: Have you done all these things at God's Word? Consider this now. Have you preached the Gospel? Was it the Gospel? Was it Christ you preached or merely something about Christ? Did you give the people bread, or did you give them plates to put the bread on and knives to cut the bread with? Did you give them water to drink, or did you give them the cup that had been near the water? Some preaching is not Gospel; it is a knife that smells of the cheese, but it is not cheese. See to that matter.

If you preached the Gospel, did you preach it properly? That is to say, did you state it affectionately, earnestly, clearly, plainly? If you preach the Gospel using great big university words and dictionary words, everyday people will be lost while they are trying to find out what your frame of reference is. You cannot expect God to bless you unless you preach the Gospel in a very simple way. Have you preached the truth lovingly with all your heart? Have you thrown yourself into it, as if the most important thing to you was the conversion of those you taught? Has prayer been mixed with it? Have you gone into the pulpit without prayer? Have you come out of it without prayer? Have you been to Sunday school without prayer? Have you come away from it without prayer? If so, since you failed to ask for the blessing, you must not wonder if you did not get it.

And another question: Has there been an example to back your teaching? Brothers, have you lived as you have preached? Sisters, have you lived as you have taught in your classes? These are questions we ought to answer, because perhaps God can reply to us, "No, you have not done according to My Word. It was not My Gospel you preached. You were a thinker, and you thought out your own thoughts, and I never promised to bless your thoughts but only My revealed truth. You spoke without love; you tried to glorify yourself by your oratory. You did not care whether souls were saved or not."

Or, suppose that God can point to you and say, "Your example was contrary to your teaching. You looked one way, but you pulled another way." In that case, there is no integrity in your prayer, is there? Come, let us change our ways. Let us try to rise to the highest pitch of obedience by the help of God's Spirit, not so that we can merit success, but so that we can command it if we act according to God's word. In the third chapter of 1 Corinthians the apostle Paul wrote that he had planted the seeds of the Gospel, his coworker Apollos had watered them, but that only God had given the increase.

And now, let me consider individual churches. I wish that the following questions would be examined by the membership of every church—especially of those churches that are not prospering: Do we as a church acknowledge the headship of Christ? Do we acknowledge the Statute Book of Christ—the one Book that alone and by itself is the religion of a Christian? Do we as a church seek the glory of God? Is that our main and only purpose? Are we travailing in birth (Gal. 4:19) for the souls of the people who live near us? Are we using every scriptural means to enlighten them with the Gospel? Are we a holy people? Is our example such that our neighbors may follow? Do we endeavor, even in the common things of life, to *"do all to the glory of God"* (1 Cor. 10:31)? Are we prayerful? (Oh, the many churches that give up their prayer meetings, because prayer is not in them! How can they expect a blessing?) Are we united? Oh, beloved, it is a horrible thing when church members talk against one another and even slander one another, as though they were enemies rather than friends. Can God bless such a church as that? Let us search throughout the camp, lest there be an Achan, whose stolen gold wedge and Babylonian garment, hidden in his tent, binds the hands of the Almighty so that He cannot fight for His people. (See Joshua 7.) Let every church see to itself in this.

Next, I address Christian people who have fallen into trouble through serving God. I am pressing you, but I want to ask you a few questions. Are you quite sure that you have served God? You know there are people who indulge eccentricities and whims and fancies. God has not promised to support you in your whims. Certain people are obstinate and will not submit to what everybody must bear who has to earn his bread in a world like this. If you are a mere mule, and get the stick, I must leave you to your reward; but I speak to people of understanding. Be as stern as a Puritan against everything that is wrong, but be supple and yielding to everything that involves self-denial on your part. God will bear us through if the quarrel is His quarrel. But if it is our own quarrel, why then, we may help ourselves. There is a big difference between being pigheaded and being steadfast. To be steadfast, as a matter of principle concerning truth that is taught by God's Word, is one thing. However, to get an odd idea into your head and stubbornly hold to it is quite another.

Besides, some men are conscientious about certain things but do not have an all-around conscience. Certain folks are conscientious about resting on the Sabbath, but the other half of the command is, *"Six days shalt thou labour"* (Exod. 20:9), and they do not remember that portion of the Law. I like a conscience that works fairly and impartially. But if your conscience gives way for the sake of your own gain or pleasure, the world will think that it is a sham, and they will not be far from the mark. However, if, through conscientiousness, you should be a sufferer, God will bear you through. Only examine and see that your conscience is enlightened by the Spirit of God.

The Way of Salvation

And now I want to address the seeking sinner. Some are longing to find peace but cannot reach it, and I want them to examine whether they have been negligent in some points, so that they are unable to say with Elijah, *"I have done all these things at thy word."*

You cannot be saved by your works. There is nothing you can do to deserve mercy. Salvation must be the free gift of God. But this is the point. God will give pardon to a sinner and peace to a troubled heart along certain lines.

Are you wholly on those lines? If so, you will have peace. And if you do not have that peace, something or other has been omitted.

Faith

The first thing is faith. Do you believe that Jesus Christ is the Son of God? Do you believe that He has risen from the dead? Do you entrust yourself wholly, simply, heartily, once for all, to Him? Then it is written, *"He that believeth on me hath everlasting life"* (John 6:47). Go and plead that.

Repentance

"I have no peace," says one. Have you sincerely repented of sin? Is your mind totally changed about sin, so that what you once loved you now hate, and what you once hated you now love? Have you had a wholehearted loathing, and giving up, and forsaking of sin? Do not deceive yourself. You cannot be saved *in* your sins; you are to be saved *from* your sins. You and your sins must part, or else Christ and you will never be joined. See to this. Labor to give up every sin and turn from every false way. Otherwise, your faith is only a dead faith, and will never save you.

Restitution

It may be that you have wronged a person and have never made restitution. Mr. D. L. Moody did great good when he preached restitution. If you have wronged another, you ought to make it up to him. You ought to return what you have stolen, if that is your sin. A person cannot expect peace of conscience until, as far as in him lies, he has made amends for any wrong he has done to his fellowman. See to that, or else, perhaps, this stone may lie at your door, and, because it is not rolled away, you may never enter into peace.

Prayer

It may be, my friend, that you have neglected prayer. Now, prayer is one of those things without which no one can find the Lord. That is how we seek Him, and if we do not seek Him, how will we find Him? If you have been neglectful in this matter of prayer, you cannot say, *"I have done all these things at thy word."* May the Lord stir you up to pray mightily, stir you up so that, like Jacob, you will not let Him go until He blesses you! As you wait on the Lord, He will cause you to find rest for your soul.

Good Associations

Possibly, however, you may be a believer in Christ, and you may have no peace because you are associated with ungodly people, going with them to their follies, and mixing with them in their amusements. You see that you cannot serve God and mammon (Matt. 6:24).

Come out from among them, and be ye separate, saith the Lord, and touch not the unclean thing; and I will receive you, and will be a Father unto you, and ye shall be my sons and daughters, saith the Lord Almighty.   *(2 Cor. 6:17–18)*

There is a certain man I know, and I am persuaded that the only thing that keeps him from Christ is the company with which he mingles. I will not say that his company is bad in itself, but it is bad for him. If there is anything that is right in itself, yet becomes ruinous to us, we must give it up. We are not commanded to cut off warts and growths. In the fifth chapter of Matthew, Jesus commands us to cut off right arms and to pluck out right eyes—good things in themselves—if they are stumbling blocks in our way so that we cannot reach Christ.

What is there in the world that is worth keeping if it means the loss of my soul? Away with it. Consequently, there are many things that are lawful to another person, but for you they may not be expedient because they would be injurious. Many things cause no harm to the majority of men, and yet to one individual they would be the most perilous things, and therefore he should avoid them. Be a law to yourselves, and stay clear of everything that keeps you away from the Savior.

Obedient in Everything

Perhaps, however, you say, "Well, as far as I know, I do keep out of all bad associations, and I am trying to follow the Lord." Let me press you with a question close to home: Will you be obedient to Jesus in everything?

> For know—nor of the terms complain—
> Where Jesus comes he comes to reign.

If you want to have Christ as your Savior, you must also take Him as your King. It is for this reason that He stresses to you, *"He that believeth and is baptized shall be saved"* (Mark 16:16). Will baptism save you? Assuredly not, for you have no right to be baptized until you are saved by faith in Jesus Christ. However, remember, if Christ gives you the command— if you accept Him as your King—you are bound to obey Him.

If, instead of saying, "Be baptized," He had simply said, "Put a feather in your cap," you might have asked, "Will putting a feather in my cap save me?" No, but you would be bound to do it if He commanded you. If He had said, "Put a stone in your pocket, and carry it with you," if that were Christ's command, you would need to take the stone and carry it with you. Often, the less importance there seems to be about a command, the more there is that hinges on it.

I have seen a rebellious boy, to whom his father has said, "Son, pick up that stick. Pick up that stick." There is no very great importance about the command, and so the youth sullenly refuses to obey. "Do you hear, son? Pick up that stick." No, he will not. Now, if it had been a great thing that he had been asked to do, which was somewhat beyond his power, it would not have been so clear an evidence of his rebellion when he refused to do it, as it was when it was only a little and trifling thing, and yet he refused to obey. Therefore, I lay great stress on this: You who do believe in Jesus Christ should act according to His Word. Say, "Lord, what would You have me do? No matter what it is, I will do it, for I am Your servant." I want you, if you desire to be Christ's, to be just like the brave men who rode at Balaclava:

"[Yours] not to reason why; / [Yours] but to do and die"—if need be, if Jesus calls you to that. Let this be your song:

> Through floods and flames if Jesus lead,
> I'll follow where he goes.

The kind of faith that at the very outset cries, "I will not do that; it is not essential," and then goes on to say, "I do not agree with that, and I do not agree with the other," is no faith at all. In that case it is you who are master and not Christ. In His own house you are beginning to alter His commands. "Oh," says one, "but as to baptism, I was baptized, you know, a great many years ago, when I was an infant." Do you say so?

You have heard of Mary, whose mistress said, "Mary, go into the drawing room, and sweep it and dust it." Her mistress went into the drawing room and found it dusty. "Mary, did you not sweep the room, and dust it?" she asked. "Well, ma'am, yes, I did. Only, I dusted it first, and then I swept it." That was the wrong order and spoiled the whole thing. And it will never do to put Christ's commands backwards, because then they mean practically nothing. We ought to do what He commands us, exactly as He commands us, when He commands us, in the order in which He commands us. It is ours simply to be obedient. When we are, we may remember that to believe Christ and to obey Christ is the same thing, and that often in Scripture the same word that might be read "believe" might also be read "obey."

He is the Author of eternal salvation to all who obey Him (Heb. 5:9), and that is to all who believe in Him. Trust Him, then, with your whole heart, and obey Him very willingly. You can then go to Him in your dying hour and say, "Lord, I have done all these things at Your Word. I claim no merit, but I do claim that You keep Your gracious promise to me, for You cannot go back on one word that You have spoken."

God bless you, beloved, for Christ's sake.

Chapter 4

Love's Law and Life

If ye love me, keep my commandments.
—John 14:15

The fourteenth chapter of John is singularly full of certainties, and remarkably studded with *ifs*. Concerning most of the great things in this chapter, there never can be an *if;* and yet, the word *if* comes up, I think, no less than seven times in the chapter, not about trifles, but about the most solemn subjects. It is, perhaps, worthy of mention that there is something connected with each of these *ifs*— something that results from it or appears to be involved in it or linked with it.

Look at verse two:

In my Father's house are many mansions:
if it were not so, I would have told you.

If there were no place for us in the glory land, Jesus would have told us. If any truth that has not been revealed would make our hope a folly, our Lord Jesus would have warned us of it, for He has not come to lure us into a fool's paradise and to deceive us in the end. He will tell us all that it is necessary for us to know for a wise faith and a sure hope.

The Lord has *"not spoken in secret, in a dark place of the earth"* (Isa. 45:19). He has not spoken in contradiction to His revealed Word. Nothing in His secret decrees or hidden designs can shake our confidence or darken our expectation. *"If it were not so, I would have told you."* If there were a secret thing that would injure your prospects, it would have been dragged to light, so that you might not be deceived, for the Lord Jesus has no desire to win disciples by the suppression of distasteful truth. If there were anything yet to be revealed that would render your hope a delusion at the end, you would have been made acquainted with it. Jesus Himself would break the sad news to you. He would not leave you to be horrified by finding it out for yourself. He kindly declares, *"I would have told you."*

Notice the third verse. Again we meet with an *if* and its consequence:

If I go and prepare a place for you, I will come again, and receive you unto myself.

If the Lord Jesus should go away (and this is a supposition no longer, for He has gone), then He would return in due time. Since He has gone, He will come again, for He has made the one to depend on the other. We do not question that He went up into heaven, for He rose up from out of the circle of His followers, and they saw Him as He went up into heaven. They had no doubt at all regarding the fact that the cloud had received Him out of their sight. Moreover, they had received assurance out of heaven, by an angelic messenger, that He *"shall so come in like manner as ye have seen him go into heaven"* (Acts 1:11). His homegoing pledges Him to come and compels us to look for Him. *"If I go and prepare a place for you, I will come again, and receive you unto myself."*

The next *if* comes at the beginning of the seventh verse:

> *If ye had known me, ye should have known my Father also.*

If we really do know the Lord Christ, we know God. In fact, there is no way to know God correctly except through His Son Jesus. It is evidently true that men do not hold to pure and simple theism for long. If men well versed in science get away from the Christ, the incarnate God, before long they drift away from God altogether. They begin to slide down the mountain when they abandon the incarnate Deity, and there is no longer any foothold to stop them.

No man comes to the Father but by the Son (John 14:6), and no man keeps to the Father very long who does not also keep to his faith in the Son. Those who know Christ, know God. But those who are ignorant of the Savior are ignorant of God, however much they may pride themselves on their religion. They may know another god, but the only living and true God is unknown except by those who receive Jesus. The divine Fatherhood, of which we hear so much in certain quarters, is only to be seen through the window of incarnation and sacrifice. We must see Jesus before we can gain even so much as a glimpse at the Infinite, the Incomprehensible, and the Invisible. God does not come within finite perception until He enters human flesh; and there we see His glory, *"full of grace and truth"* (John 1:14).

You will find the next *if* a little farther down in the chapter, in the fourteenth verse:

If ye shall ask any thing in my name, I will do it.

The *if* in this case involves an uncertainty about our prayers—if there is an uncertainty at all. Taking it for granted that we do ask for mercies in the name of Jesus, a glorious certainty is linked to it. Jesus says, *"I will do it."* Here our Lord speaks in a sovereign style. We may not say, "I will." The "I wills" pertain to Christ. He can answer, and He has the right to answer. Therefore, He says without reservation, "I will": *"If ye shall ask any thing in my name, I will do it."*

Oh, that we might put the first *if* out of consideration by continually petitioning the Lord and signing our petitions with the name of Jesus! May we be persistent only in prayers to which we are authorized to attach the words "in Jesus' name." Then, boldly using His name and authority, we will not need to be under any apprehension of failure. The great Father in heaven never denies the power of His Son's name. Neither does the Son Himself draw back from keeping His own pledges. True prayer operates with the same certainty as the laws of nature. *"Delight thyself also in the LORD; and he shall give thee the desires of thine heart"* (Ps. 37:4). Oh, if only we delighted more in the divine name and character, then our prayers would always speed to the throne!

In the fifteenth verse we discover the *if* of our text, of which I will say nothing for the moment: *"If ye love me, keep my commandments."* Something, you see, is to come out of this *if*, the same as out of all the others. *If* something, *then* something: *"If ye love me"* then carry it out to the legitimate result, which is *"keep my commandments."*

You will find the next *if* in the twenty-third verse:

> *Jesus answered and said unto him, If a man love me, he will keep my words.*

Respect for His wisdom and obedience to His authority will grow out of love. *"The love of Christ constraineth us"* (2 Cor. 5:14). We often hear people quote that passage as, "The love of Christ *ought to* constrain us," but that is a corruption of the text. The apostle tells us that the love of Christ does constrain us. And if it really enters the heart, it will do so. It is an active, moving power, influencing the inner life and then the external conduct.

'Tis love that makes our willing feet
In swift obedience move.

"If a man love me, he will keep my words." He will believe in the verbal inspiration of his Lord; he will regard His teaching as infallible; he will attend to it and remember it. More

than this, he will, by his conduct, carry out the words of his Lord, and therefore he will keep them in the best possible manner by enshrining them in his daily life.

The chapter almost closes at the twenty-eighth verse with:

> *If ye loved me, ye would rejoice, because I said, I go unto the Father: for my Father is greater than I.*

When we have an intelligent love for Christ, we rejoice in His gains even though we ourselves appear to be the losers as a result. The physical absence of our Lord from our midst might seem to us to be a great loss, but we rejoice in it because it is for His own greater glory. If He is enthroned in glory, we do not dare lament His absence. Our love agrees to His departure, even rejoices in it, for anything that contributes to His exaltation is sweet to us. Let us, at this moment, because we love Him, rejoice that He has gone to the Father.

So, if you read the fourteenth chapter of John, you see that, though it is enriched with heavenly certainties, it is also sprinkled with *if*s. Like little pools of sparkling water among the ever abiding rocks, these *if*s gleam in the light of heaven and refresh us even to look upon them.

Let us now consider our text, and may the Holy Spirit lead us into the secret chambers of it!

If ye love me, keep my commandments.

We will look at three aspects of this verse. Initially, we will see that the *if* we are considering now is a serious one. Then we will discover that the test that is added concerning it is a very judicious one: *"Keep my commandments."* And we will come to see that this test will be endured by love, for the words are translated in the Revised Version (RV): *"Ye will keep my commandments."* Obedience will follow love as a matter of certainty.

A Very Serious *If*

The *if* in this verse is a very serious one because it goes to the very root of the matter. Love belongs to the heart, and every surgeon will tell you that a disease of the heart may not be trifled with. A gifted doctor said to me, "I feel at ease with any matter if it does not concern the head or the heart." Solomon charged us: *"Keep thy heart with all diligence; for out of it are the issues of life"* (Prov. 4:23). If the mainspring fails, all the works of a watch refuse to act. We cannot, therefore, think little of a question that concerns our love, for it deals with a vital part of us. O friends, I hope there is no question about your love for Jesus.

Observe how our Savior puts this *if* in such a way as to teach us that love must be prior to obedience. The text is not, "Keep my commandments, and then love me." No, we do not expect pure streams until the fountain is cleansed. Nor does He say, "Keep my commandments, and love me at the same time," as two separate things, although that might correspond with truth in some measure. But love is put first, because it is first in importance and first in experience. *"If ye love me"*—we must begin with love—then *"keep my commandments."*

Love must act as mother, nurse, and food to obedience. The essence of obedience lies in the hearty love that prompts the deed, rather than in the deed itself. I can imagine that a person might, in his outward life, keep Christ's commandments; and yet he might never keep them at all in such a way as to be accepted before God. If he became obedient by compulsion, but would disobey if he dared, then his heart is not right before God, and his actions are of little worth. The commandments are to be kept out of love for Him who gave them.

In the realm of obedience, to love is to live: if we love Christ, we will live for Christ. Love for the person of our Lord is the very salt of our sacrifices. To put it in very practical terms, I often say to myself, "Today I have performed all the duties of my office. But have I been careful to remain in my Lord's love? I have not failed to do all that was possible for me. I have gone from early morning until late at night, packing as much work as possible into every hour and trying to do it with all my heart. But have I, after all, done this as unto the Lord and for His sake?" I tremble for fear that I should serve God merely because I happen to be a minister and am called to preach His Word or because the natural routine of the day carries me through it. I am concerned that I may not be impelled by any force but the love of Jesus. This fear often humbles me in the dust and prevents all glorying in what I have done.

Only as we love our Lord can our obedience be true and acceptable. The main concern of our lives should be to do what is right because we love the Lord. We must walk *before* the Lord as Abraham did, and *with* the Lord as Enoch did. Unless we are under the constant constraint of love for the Lord Jesus Christ, we will fail terribly.

Knowledge, alas! is all in vain,
　And all in vain our fear,
In vain our labour and our pain
　If love be absent there.

See, dear friends, how inward true religion really is, how far it exceeds all external formalism! How deep is the seat of true grace. You cannot hope to do what Christ can smile on until your heart is renewed. A heart at enmity with God cannot be made acceptable by mere acts of piety. The main thing is not what your hands are doing, or even what your lips are saying; it is what you mean and intend in your heart. Which way are your affections tending? The great flywheel that moves the whole machinery of life is fixed in the heart. Therefore, this is the most important of all conditions: *"If ye love me."*

These words have a searching sound. I jump when I hear them. The person who believes in the Lord Jesus Christ for his salvation produces, as the first fruit of his faith, love for Christ. This love must abound in us or nothing is right. Packed away within that box of sweets called "love," you will find every holy thing. But if you have no love, what do you have? Though you wear your fingers to the bone with service, weep out your eyes with repentance, make your knees hard with kneeling, and dry your throat with shouting, if your heart does not beat with love, your religion falls to the ground like a withered leaf in autumn. Love is the chief jewel in the bracelet of obedience. Read the text, and note it well: *"If ye love me, keep my commandments."*

What a great amount of religion may be cast out as worthless by this text! Men may keep on going to church, they may be religious throughout their whole lives, and they may be apparently blameless in their moral conduct, and yet there may be nothing in them because there is no love for the ever blessed Christ at the foundation of their profession of faith.

When the heathen killed their sacrifices in order to prophesy future events from the entrails, the worst omen they ever got was when the priest, after searching into the victim, could not find a heart, or if that heart was small and shriveled. The soothsayers always declared that this omen was the sure sign of calamity. All the signs were evil if the heart of the offering was absent or deficient. This is especially true with religion and with each religious person. He who searches us, principally searches our hearts. He who tries mankind, chiefly tries the thoughts and intents of the children of men.

The Master is with us, walking with noiseless step, wearing a golden band across His breast and robed in snow-white garments down to His feet. See, He stops before each one of us and gently asks, *"Lovest thou me?"* Three times He repeats the question. (See John 21:15–17.) He waits for an answer. It is a vital question. Do not refuse a reply. Oh, that the Spirit of the Lord may enable you to answer in sincerity and truth, *"Lord, thou knowest all things; thou knowest that I love thee"* (v. 17)!

This matter of love for Jesus is put prior to every other because it is the best reason for our obedience to Him. Notice that He says, *"If ye love me, keep my commandments."* Personal affection will produce personal obedience. Do you not see the meaning of the words? The blessed Jesus says to each of us, "If you love Me, keep My commandments," because, truly, operative love is mainly love toward a person, and love toward our Lord produces obedience to His precepts.

There are some people for whom you would do anything—you want to yield to their wills. If such a person were to say to you, "Do this," you would do it without question. Perhaps a person like this is in the position of being your employer, and you serve him willingly. Perhaps he is a venerated friend, and because you esteem and love him, his word is law to you. The Savior may much more safely than any other be installed in such a position. From the throne of your affections, He says, "If you love Me—if your heart really goes out to Me—then let My Word be a commandment, let My commandment be kept in your memory, and then let it further be kept by being observed in your life."

So, do you see the reason why the Master begins with the heart? There is no hope of obedience to Him in our actions unless He is enshrined in our affections. Love for the Holy One is the spring and source of all holy living. Dear friends, have you been captured by the beauties of Jesus, and are you held in a divine captivity to the Person of your redeeming Lord, who is worthy to be adored? Then you have within you the impulse that constrains you to keep His commandments.

It was very necessary for our Lord to address His disciples in this way. Yes, it was necessary to speak in this way even to the apostles. He said to the chosen Twelve, *"If ye love me."* We would never have doubted one of them. We now know, by the outcome, that one of them was a traitor to his Lord and sold Him for pieces of silver. But no one suspected him, for he seemed as loyal as any one of them. And if that question, *"If ye love me,"* needed to be raised in the sacred college of the Twelve, how much more must it be allowed to sift our churches and to test us!

My friends, this word is extremely needed among Christians today. Hear its voice: *"If ye love me."* The mixed multitude of people in our churches may be compared to the heap on the threshing floor that John the Baptist described in the third chapter of Matthew. The winnowing fan is clearly needed. Perhaps you have almost taken it for granted that you love Jesus, but it must not be taken for granted. Some of you have been born into a religious atmosphere, you have lived in the midst of godly people, and you have never been out into the wicked world to be tempted by its follies. Therefore, you have come to the careless conclusion that you must assuredly love the Lord. This is unwise and perilous. Never glory in armor that you have not tested, or rejoice in love for Christ that has not been tried and proven. What an awful thing if you should be deceived and mistaken!

It is most kind of the Savior to raise a question about your love, and therefore to give you an opportunity to examine yourself and see whether your heart is right. It would be far better for you to err on the side of too much anxiety than on that of carnal security. To be afraid that you are wrong, and therefore to make sure of being right, will bring you to a far better end than being sure that you are right and therefore refusing to examine the ground of your hope. I want you to be fully assured of your love for Jesus, but I do not want you to be deceived by a belief that you have Him if you do not. *"Search me, O God, and know my heart: try me, and know my thoughts"* (Ps. 139:23).

Remember, if anyone does not love the Lord Jesus Christ, he will be *"Anathema Maranatha"* (1 Cor. 16:22), cursed at His coming. This applies to everyone, even though he may be very eminent. An apostle turned out to be a *"son of perdition"* (John 17:12)—may not you? Any man, even though he may be a learned bishop, a popular pastor, a renowned evangelist, a venerable elder, an active deacon, or the most ancient member of the most orthodox congregation, may yet turn out not to be a lover of the Lord. Though he has gathered to break bread in the sacred name with a select company, if he does not truly love the Lord Jesus Christ, the curse rests on him, whoever he may be. So let us, right now, take from the Master's mouth the heart-searching word, *"If ye love me, keep my commandments."* Let us take it to heart, as if it is addressed to each one of us, personally and alone.

While you are considering this verse, do not compare yourself with others. What do you have to do in this matter with keeping the vineyards of others? See to your own heart. The text does not say, "If the church loves me," or, "If such and such a minister loves me," or, "If your brothers love me," but it is, *"If ye love me, keep my commandments."* The most important questions for each one to answer are those concerning his personal attachment to his Redeemer and the personal obedience that comes out of it.

I press this inquiry upon you. It may seem like a trite and commonplace question, but it needs to be put again and again before all people in our churches. The preacher needs to be questioned in this way, for he gets into the habit of reading his Bible for other people. The Sunday school teacher needs this inquiry, for he also is apt to study the Scriptures for his class rather than for himself. We all need the truth to come home to us with personal and forcible application, for we are always inclined to shift unpleasant inquiries onto others. When we are conversing with very deaf people, we speak right into their ears, and I wish to address you in a similar way, so that it hits home pointedly to you at this time. Let the text reverberate in your ear and mind and heart: *"If ye love me, keep my commandments."*

The question is answerable, however. It was put to the apostles, and they could answer

it. Peter spoke as all the eleven would have
when he said, *"Thou knowest that I love thee"*
(John 21:17). It is not a question concerning
mysteries that are out of range and beyond
judgment. It deals with a plain matter of fact. A
person can know whether he loves the Lord or
not, and he ought to know. Yet, the person who
watchfully guards himself, and is, therefore,
half afraid to speak positively, may all the more
truly be a lover of the Lord. Holy caution in the
heart of someone like this may raise a question
where the answer is far more certain than in
the hearts of those who never even make the
inquiry because they are carnally secure.

Do not be content with merely longing to
love Jesus or with longing to know whether you
love Him. Not to know whether you love the
Lord Jesus is a state of mind so dangerous that I
exhort you never to go to sleep until you have
escaped from it. A man has no right to smile—I
had almost written, he has no right to eat bread
or drink water—as long as that question hangs
in the balance. It ought to be decided. It can be
decided. It can be decided at once.

Not love Jesus? It would be better for me
not to live than not to love Him. Not love
Christ? May the terrible fact never be hidden
from my weeping eyes! Perhaps the dread dis-
covery may drive me to better things. If I do

love my Lord, I can never rest with the shadow
of a doubt darkening the life of my love. A
question on such a matter is unbearable.

> Do not I love thee from my soul?
>   Then let me nothing love:
> Dead be my heart to every joy,
>   When Jesus cannot move.

> Would not my heart pour forth its blood
>   In honour of thy name,
> And challenge the cold hand of death
>   To damp the immortal flame?

> Thou know'st I love thee, dearest Lord;
>   But oh, I long to soar
> Far from the sphere of mortal joys,
>   And learn to love thee more.

My friends, hear the question suggested by this
little word, *if.* Consider it well, and do not rest
until you can say, *"I love the LORD, because he
hath heard my voice and my supplications"*
(Ps. 116:1).

So much, then, concerning the serious nature of this *if.*

A Judicious *If*

Let me further observe that the test that
is proposed in the text is a very judicious one:

115

"*Keep my commandments.*" This is the best proof of love.

The test indicated does not suggest a lawless liberty. It is true that we are "*not under the law, but under grace*" (Rom. 6:14). But we are still "*under the law to Christ*" (1 Cor. 9:21); and if we love Him, we are to keep His commandments. Let us never enter into the counsel of those who do not believe that there are any commandments for believers to keep. Those who do away with duty, do away with sin, and, consequently, do away with the Savior. It is not written, "If ye love me, do whatever you please." Jesus does not say, "As long as you love me in your hearts, I do not care anything about your lives." There is no such doctrine as that between the covers of the Holy Book. He who loves Christ is the freest person outside of heaven, but he is also the most under bonds. He is free, for Christ has loosed his bonds, but he is put under bonds to Christ by grateful love. The love of Christ constrains him, from this time forward, to live for the Lord who loved him, lived for him, died for him, and rose again for him.

No, dear friends, we do not desire a lawless life. He who is not under the law as a power for condemnation can yet say that with his heart he delights in the law of God (Rom. 7:22). He longs for perfect holiness, and in his soul he yields heartfelt homage to the precepts of the Lord Jesus. Love is law; the law of love is the strongest of all laws. Christ has become our Master and King, and *"his commandments are not grievous"* (1 John 5:3).

Also, our text does not contain any fanatical challenge. We do not read, "If you love Me, perform some extraordinary act." The test required is not an outburst of extravagance or an attempt to realize the ambitious project of a feverish brain. It is nothing of the kind. Hermits, nuns, and religious madcaps find no example or precept here. Some people think that if they love Jesus, they must enter a convent, retire to a cell, dress themselves oddly, or shave their heads. Some men have thought, "If we love Christ, we must strip ourselves of everything we possess, put on sackcloth, tie ropes around our waists, and pine away in the desert." Others have thought it wise to make themselves look absurd by odd dress and behavior. The Savior does not say anything of the kind. Rather, He says, *"If ye love me, keep my commandments."*

Every now and then, we find members of our churches who feel they must leave their trades and their callings to show their love for Jesus. Their children may starve, and their wives may waste away, but their mad whimsies must be carried out for "love of Jesus." Under this influence they rush into all sorts of foolish behavior and soon ruin their reputations, because they will not take the advice of sobriety and cannot be satisfied with the grand test of love that our Lord Himself lays down in this verse. The text does not condemn these frivolous projects specifically, but it does so in general by proposing a more reasonable test: *"If ye love me, keep my commandments."*

Do not spin theories in your excited brain and vow that you will do this desperate thing or the other. The probability is that you are not seeking the glory of the Lord but that you are desiring fame for yourself. You are aiming at supreme devotion so that you may become a distinguished person and so people may talk about your superior sainthood. You may even go so far as to court persecution from selfish motives. The Savior, who is wise, knows what is in men, and He also knows what is the surest test of true love for Himself: *"If ye love me, keep my commandments."* This is a much more difficult thing than to follow out the dictates of a crazy mind.

Why does the Savior give us this as a test? I think that one reason is because it proves whether you love Christ in His true position or whether your love is for a christ of your own making and your own placing. It is easy to want a half-christ and to refuse a whole Christ. It is also easy to follow a christ of your own making, who is merely an antichrist. The real Christ is so great and glorious that He has a right to give commandments. Moses never used an expression such as our Savior employs here. Moses might have said, "Keep God's commandments," but he never would have said, "Keep my commandments." That dear and divine person whom we call Master and Lord says here, *"Keep my commandments."* What a commanding person He must be! What lordship He has over His people! How great He is among His saints! If you keep His commandments, you are putting Him into the position that He claims. By your obedience you confess His sovereignty and divinity, and you say with Thomas, *"My Lord and my God"* (John 20:28).

I am afraid that a great many people know a christ who is meek and lowly, their servant and Savior, but they do not know the *Lord* Jesus Christ. Alas! My friends, such people set up a false christ. We do not love Jesus at all if He is not our Lord and God. It is all whining pretension and hypocrisy, this love for Christ that robs Him of His deity. I abhor that love for

Christ that does not make Him King of Kings, and Lord of Lords. Love Him, yet belittle Him? It is absurd. Follow your own will in preference to His will, and then talk of love for Him? Ridiculous! This is only the Devil's counterfeit of love. It is a contradiction of all true love. Love is loyal and crowns its Lord with obedience. If you love Jesus properly, you view His every precept as a divine commandment. You love the true Christ if you love a commanding Christ as well as a saving Christ, and if you look to Him to guide your life as well as to pardon your sin.

This test, again, is very judicious, because it proves the living presence of the object of your love. Love always desires to have its object near, and it has an ability to bring its object near. If you love someone, that person may be far away, and yet to your thoughts he is close at hand. Love brings the beloved one so near that the thought of this beloved one exerts influence over a person's life.

Suppose that a gentleman has faithful servants. He goes away and leaves his house in their charge. Even though he has gone abroad, he is at home to his servants, for every day their work is done as if he were there to see it. He is coming home soon, they hardly know when, but they keep all things in readiness for his return, let it happen when it may. They are not "eye" servants, who only attend to their duty when watched, and therefore they do not work any less because he is absent. Even if he does not see them, the eyes of their love always see him, and therefore they work as if he were at home. Their affection keeps him always near.

Imagine that a dear father has died, and has left his property to a son who honors his memory. What does the son do? He is generous, like his father. When he is asked why, he replies, "I do exactly what I believe my dear father would do if he were here." Again, he is asked why. He answers, "Because I love him."

When a man is dead, he is still alive to those who love him. In the same manner, the living Christ, who is not dead but has gone away, is made present to us by our real love. The proof of our love is that Jesus is so present that He constrains our actions, influences our motives, and is the cause of our obedience. Jesus seems to be saying, "If you love Me, now that I am gone you will do as you would have done if I were still with you and looking at you. You will continue to keep My commandments as you would in My presence."

It is a most judicious test, once again, because, by keeping our Lord's commandments, we are doing what is most pleasing to Him and will most glorify Him. Some enthusiastic Methodist may cry,

Oh, what shall I do my Saviour to praise?

To him I would say, "Listen carefully, my brother. If you love your Savior, keep His commandments. This is all you have to do, and it is a great 'all,' too. Among the rest of His commandments, you may come and be baptized, while you are so earnest to praise your Lord."

"If ye love me, keep my commandments." There is the answer to every rapturous inquiry. Jesus is more glorified by a consistent obedience to His commands than by the most extravagant zeal that we can possibly display. That is only man-made worship because He has never commanded it. If you wish to break the alabaster box and fill the house with sweet perfume, as Mary anointed Jesus in the twelfth chapter of John, and if you wish to crown His head with rarest gems, the method is before you: *"Keep my commandments."* You cannot do your Lord a greater favor or, in the long run, bring to Him more real an honor than by rendering complete, continual, hearty obedience to every one of His commandments.

Moreover, the Savior knew, when He instructed us to prove this test, that it would prepare us for honoring and glorifying Him in all other ways. Read the context:

If ye love me, keep my commandments. And I will pray the Father, and he shall give you another Comforter, that he may abide with you for ever.   (John 14:15–16)

You can greatly glorify Christ if you are filled with the Holy Spirit, but you cannot be filled with the Holy Spirit if you do not keep Christ's commandments. The Spirit of God as Comforter will come only to those to whom He comes as Sanctifier. By making us holy, He will qualify us for being useful. The Savior says, "If ye love me, keep my commandments," because we will then obtain that divine Gift by which we can glorify His name. If there is any service to which your love would aspire, obedience to your Lord is the way to it.

But, indeed, I do not need to argue this. When your friend is dying and he asks you to prove your love by such and such a deed, he may ask whatever he will; you give him carte blanche. It may be the simplest thing or the hardest thing, but if he prescribes it as a test of love, you will not refuse him. Or, if your wife says to you, "You are going to journey far from

me, and I will not see you again for many days.
I beg you, therefore, to carry my picture with
you," you would not fail to do so. It would be a
simple thing, but it would be sacred to you.
Baptism and the Lord's Supper will never be
slighted by those whose hearts are fully possessed with love for Jesus. They may seem like
trifles, but if the Lord Jesus commands them,
they cannot be neglected. To stop wearing your
wedding ring might be no great crime, and yet
no loving wife would do it. In the same way,
none who regard outward ordinances as love
tokens will think of neglecting them. It is not
ours to ask for reasons, not ours to dispute
about whether the deed is essential or nones-
sential; it is only ours to obey very lovingly.
Bridegroom of our hearts, say what You will,
and we will obey You! If You will smile and
strengthen us, nothing will be impossible if it
is great, and nothing will be considered trifling
if it is small.

A Compelling *If*

I pray that God will prove the truth of this
next statement to you, which is: True love will
endure the test. *"If ye love me, ye will keep my
commandments."* Again, I have used the
translation from the Revised Version here, and

I hope it will be written out in capital letters on our revised lives! We will obey, we must obey, since we love Him by whom the command is given.

So then, beloved, let me say this much to you: If you love Christ, set to work to find out what His commandments are. Study the Scriptures regarding every point upon which you have the slightest question. This Sacred Oracle must guide you.

Next, always be true to your convictions about what Christ's commandments are. Carry them out at all costs, and carry them out at once. It would be wicked to say, "Up to this point, I have obeyed, but I will stop here." We are committed to implicit obedience to all of the Master's will, regardless of what it involves. Will you not agree to this at the outset? If you love Him, you will not hesitate.

Also, take note of every commandment as it personally concerns you. Let me mention several commandments, and beg you to obey them as you hear them. *"Go ye into all the world, and preach the gospel to every creature"* (Mark 16:15). Is this not a call to some of you to be missionaries? Do you hear it? Will you not say, *"Here am I; send me"* (Isa. 6:8)?

Perhaps you are full of enmity; somebody has treated you very badly, and you cannot forget it. I urge you to hear the Lord's command: *"Little children...love one another"* (John 13:33–34). And again:

> *Therefore if thou bring thy gift to the altar,*
> *and there rememberest that thy brother*
> *hath ought against thee; leave there thy*
> *gift before the altar, and go thy way; first*
> *be reconciled to thy brother, and then come*
> *and offer thy gift.* (Matt. 5:23–24)

If you are in debt, obey this commandment: *"Owe no man any thing, but to love one another"* (Rom. 13:8). If you neglect the poor, and live in a stingy way, hear this commandment: *"Give to him that asketh thee, and from him that would borrow of thee turn not thou away"* (Matt. 5:42). Behind everything is this: *"If ye love me, keep my commandments."* I might mention, one after another, commandments that would be especially applicable, but I pray that the Holy Spirit will *"bring all things to your remembrance"* (John 14:26).

If there is a commandment that you do not relish, it ought to be a warning to you that there is something wrong in your heart that needs to be set right. If you ever quarrel with one of Christ's commands, end that quarrel by especially attending to it beyond every other. Do as the miserly man did when he conquered his greed once and for all. He was a Christian, and he promised he would give a pound to the church. But the Devil whispered, "You need your money. Do not pay." The man stamped his foot and said, "I will give two." Then the Devil said, "Surely you are going mad. Save your money." The man replied that he would not be conquered, that he would give four pounds. "Now," said Satan, "You must be insane." Then the man said, "I will give eight. And if you don't stop your tempting, I will give sixteen, for I will not be the slave of covetousness." The point is to throw your whole soul into that very duty in which you are most tempted to be slack. Jesus does not say, "If ye love me, keep this commandment or that," but, "Out of love, obey every command."

Some of you do not love my Lord Jesus Christ. I have not directed this topic to you, but that very fact should make you thoughtful. Consider that I have had nothing to say to you because you do not love the Lord Jesus Christ and therefore cannot keep His commandments. Write down in black and white: "I do not love the Lord Jesus Christ." If this is really so, be honest enough to make a note of it, and think it over. If you love Jesus, you may joyfully write out, "I love the Lord Jesus. Oh, for grace to love Him more!" But if you do not love Him, it will be the honest thing to put it on record. Write it boldly: "I do not love the Lord Jesus Christ." Look at it, and look again. May God the Holy Spirit lead you to repent of not loving Jesus, who is the altogether lovely One and the great Lover of men's souls! Oh, that you may begin to love Him at once!

Chapter 5

The Friends of Jesus

*Ye are my friends, if ye do whatsoever
I command you.*
—John 15:14

Our Lord Jesus Christ is beyond comparison the best of all friends—a friend in need, a friend indeed. "Friend!" said Socrates, "there is no friend!" But Socrates did not know our Lord Jesus, or he would have added, "except the Savior." In the heart of our Lord Jesus there burns such friendship toward us that all other forms of it are as dim candles to the sun. *"Greater love hath no man than this, that a man lay down his life for his friends"* (John 15:13).

An ordinary man has gone as far as he possibly can when he has died for his friend. Yet he would have died anyhow, so that in dying for his friend he merely pays, somewhat beforehand, a debt that inevitably must have been discharged. With Christ, there was no need to die at all, and this, therefore, places only His love and His friendship by itself. He, who did not need to die, died, and died in agony when He might have lived in glory. Never did man give such proof of friendship as this.

Let our Lord's friendship to us be the model of our friendship to Him. It cannot be so in all respects, because our situations and conditions are different. His must always be the love of the greater to the lesser, the love of the benefactor to one in need, the love of the Redeemer to those who are bought with a price. However, the whole tone and spirit of our Lord's friendship is such that the more closely we can imitate it the better. Such friendship as His should be reflected in a friendship most hearty and self-sacrificing on our part.

In this text from John 15, our Lord does not, I think, speak to us about His being our friend, but about our being His friends. He is the friend of sinners. But sinners are not His friends until their hearts are changed. *"Ye are my friends, if ye do whatsoever I command you."* We are not His friends until then. His love for us is entirely of Himself, but friendship requires something from us. Friendship cannot be all on one side. One-sided friendship is more properly called mercy, grace, or benevolence. Friendship in its full sense is mutual. You may do all you please for a man and be perfectly benevolent, and yet he may give you nothing in return. However, real friendship can only exist where there is a response.

Therefore, we do not have before us the question as to whether Christ loves and pities us or not, for in another part of Scripture we read of *"his great love wherewith he loved us, even when we were dead in sins"* (Eph. 2:4–5). He befriended us when we were enemies, but that is not our subject right now. The question is about our being His friends, and this is what we must become if, indeed, there is to be any intimacy of mutual friendship. Friendship cannot be, as I have said, all on one side. It is like a pair of scales: there must be something to balance on the other side. There must be a return of kindly feeling from the person loved. Jesus tells us here that if we are to be His friends, we must do whatever He commands us, and in John 14:15, He says that we must do this out of love for Him.

Beloved, it is the highest honor in the world to be called the friend of Christ. Surely there is no title that excels in dignity that which was worn by Abraham, who was called the *"Friend of God"* (James 2:23). Lord Brooke was so delighted with the friendship of Sir

Philip Sydney that he ordered nothing but this to be engraved on his tomb: "Here lies the friend of Sir Philip Sydney." There is beauty in such a feeling, but still it is a small matter compared with being able to say, "Here lives a friend of Christ." What wondrous condescension, that He should call me "friend."

If I am indeed a true believer, not only is He my Friend, without whom I could have no hope here or hereafter, but He has, in the abundance of His grace, been pleased to regard me as His friend. He has been pleased to write down my name in the honored list of intimates who are permitted to speak familiarly with Him, as those do between whom there are no secrets. These intimate friends of Christ open their hearts completely to Him, while He hides nothing from them, saying, *"If it were not so, I would have told you"* (John 14:2).

Beloved, in what a light this sets obedience to Christ's commandments! I cannot help noticing how the doctrine of our text transforms obedience and makes it the joy and glory of life. How precious it is, for it is a better seal of friendship than the possession of the largest gifts and influence. Christ does not say, "You are My friends, if you rise to a position of respectability among men or honor in the church." No, however poor you may be—and those to whom He spoke these words were very poor—He says, *"Ye are my friends, if ye do whatsoever I command you."*

Obedience is better than wealth and better than rank. Jesus values His friends, not by what they have or what they wear, but by what they do. We may credit all of the eleven apostles with having remarkable qualifications for their life-work. Yet, their Lord does not say, "You are My friends because I have qualified you for apostleship." Even to these leaders of His sacred flock Jesus says plainly, "You are My friends, if you do whatever I command you. This is the point by which your friendship will be tested: If you are obedient, you are My friends."

He says neither less nor more to any of us today who aspire to the high dignity of being contained within the circle of His personal friendship. You must, my dear fellow believers, yield obedience to your Master and Lord and be eager to do it, or you are not His intimate friends. This is the one essential, which grace alone can give us. Do we rebel against the request? Far from it; our joy and delight lie in bearing our Beloved's easy yoke.

What Kind of Obedience?

Let us look at the subject more closely. Notice that our Lord Himself tells us what obedience He requests from those who call themselves His friends. True friends are eager to know what they can do to please the objects of their love. Let us gladly listen to what our Lord, who is worthy of adoration, speaks to the select circle of His chosen. He asks this of one and all: obedience.

None of us are exempted from doing His commandments. However lofty or however lowly your condition, you must obey. If you have only one talent, you must obey; and if you have ten, you must still obey. There can be no friendship with Christ unless we are willing, each one of us, to give Him hearty, loyal service.

Let this thought penetrate the hearts of all upon whom the name of Jesus Christ is named: If you are enrolled among the friends of Jesus, you must be careful about your own personal obedience to His blessed will. Do not forget that even to the *"queen,"* standing on His right *"in gold of Ophir,"* the word is given, *"He is thy Lord; and worship thou him"* (Ps. 45:9, 11).

Active Obedience

Also, notice that it must be active obedience. *"If ye do."* Some people think it is quite sufficient if they avoid what He forbids. Abstinence from evil is a great part of righteousness, but it is not enough for friendship. If a man can say, "I am not a drunkard, I am not dishonest, I am not unchaste, I am not a violator of the Sabbath, I am not a liar," so far so good, but such righteousness does not exceed that of the scribes and Pharisees, and they cannot enter the kingdom. It is well if you do not willfully transgress, but if you are to be Christ's friends, there must be far more than this. A person would be a poor friend if he only said, "I am your friend, and to prove it, I don't insult you, I don't rob you, I don't speak evil of you." Surely there must be more positive evidence to certify friendship.

The Lord Jesus Christ puts great stress on positive duties. At the Last Day He will say, *"I was an hungered, and ye gave me meat: I was thirsty, and ye gave me drink"* (Matt. 25:35). In that memorable twenty-fifth chapter of Matthew nothing is said about negative virtues, but positive actions are cited and dwelt on in detail. There is an old English saying, "He is my friend who grinds at my mill." That is to say, friendship shows itself in doing helpful acts that prove sincerity. Fine words are mere wind and have no value, if they are not backed up with substantial deeds of kindness. Friendship cannot live on windy talk; it needs matter-of-fact bread. The inspired Word says, "Show me proof of your love; show it by doing whatever I command you."

Continuous Obedience

In addition, it is clear, from the wording of the text, that the obedience Christ expects from us is continuous. He does not say, "If you sometimes do what I command you—if you do it on Sundays, for instance—if you do what I command you in your place of worship, that will suffice." No, we are to abide in Him and keep His statutes even to the end.

I am not now teaching works as the way of salvation but as the evidence of fellowship, which is quite another thing. We must seek, in every place, at all times, and under all circumstances, to do as Jesus commands us out of a cheerful spirit of reverence toward Him. Such tender, loving subjection, as a godly wife gives to her husband, must be gladly yielded by us throughout life if we are His friends.

Universal Obedience

This obedience must also be universal. *"Whatsoever I command you."* No sooner is anything discovered to be the subject of a command than the one who is a true friend of Christ says, "I will do it," and he does it. He does not pick and choose which precept he will keep and which he will neglect, for this is self-will and not obedience.

The Friends of Jesus

I have known some people who have professed faith in Christ to err greatly in this matter. They have been very strict over one point, and they have blamed everybody who did not come up to their strictness, talking as if that one duty fulfilled the whole law. "Straining at gnats," about which Jesus warned the scribes and Pharisees in the twenty-third chapter of Matthew, has been a preoccupation with many. They have bought a choice assortment of strainers of the very finest net to get out all the gnats from their cup, but the next day they have opened their mouths and swallowed a camel without a qualm. This will not do. The test is: *"Whatsoever I command you."*

I do not mean that little things are unimportant; far from it. If there is a gnat that Christ commands you to strain at, strain it out with great diligence. Do not let even a flea escape you if He commands you to remove it. The smallest command of Christ may often be the most important, and I will tell you why. Some things are great, obviously great, and for many reasons even a hypocritical person who professes to believe in Christ will attend to them. However, the test may lie in the minor points, which hypocrites do not take the trouble to notice, since no human tongue would praise them for doing them.

Here is the proof of your love: Will you do the smaller thing for Jesus, as well as the more weighty matter? Too many say, "I do not see any use in it; I can be saved without it; there are a great many different opinions on the point," and so on. All this comes of evil and is not consistent with the spirit of friendship with Christ, for love pleases even in trifles. Is it Christ's will? Is it plainly a precept of His Word? Then it is not yours to reason why or to raise any question.

The reality of your subjection to your Lord and Master may hinge on those seemingly insignificant points. A domestic servant might place the breakfast on the table and feel that she had done her duty. But if her mistress had told her to place the salt on the table, and she had not done so, she would be asked the cause of her neglect. Suppose she replied to her mistress, "I did not think it was necessary. I placed the breakfast before you, but a little salt was too trifling a matter for me to worry about." Her mistress might answer, "But I told you to be sure to put out the salt. Mind you do so tomorrow." The next morning there is no salt, and the maid says that she did not see the use of setting it on the table. Her mistress is displeased and tells her that her wish must be carried out. Will she not be a very foolish and

troublesome girl if she refuses to do so because
she does not see the use of it? I think it is
likely that the young woman would have to
find other employment before long, for such
conduct is very annoying.

It is the same way with those who profess
to have faith but say, "I have attended to the
main things, and what I neglect is quite a minor matter." Such are not even good servants;
friends they can never be. I implore you, dear
believers, strive for universal obedience.
"Whatsoever he saith unto you, do it" (John
2:5). Only by an earnest endeavor to carry out
all of His will can you live in happy fellowship
with Him, and indeed be His friends.

Obedience As unto the Lord

Note well that this obedience is to be rendered as if it is to Christ Himself. Put the em-
phasis on the little word *I: "Ye are my friends,
if ye do whatsoever I command you."* We are to
do these things because Jesus commands them.
Does not the royal person of our Lord cast a
very strong light on the necessity of obedience?
When we refuse to obey, we refuse to do what
the Lord Himself commands. When the Lord
Jesus Christ, the Son of God and our Redeemer, is denied obedience, it is treason. How

can rebels against the King be His Majesty's friends? The precepts of Scripture are not the commandments of man or the ordinances of angels. They are the laws of Christ, and how dare we despise them? We are to act justly because Jesus commands us to and because we love to do His pleasure. There can be no friendship without this. Oh, for grace to *"serve the LORD with gladness"* (Ps. 100:2).

Willing Obedience

Moreover, it appears that our Lord wants us to obey Him out of a friendly spirit. To obey Christ as if we were forced to do it under pains and penalties would be of no worth as a proof of friendship. Everyone can see that. He does not speak of slaves but of friends. He does not want us to perform duties out of fear of punishment or love of reward. That which He can accept from His friends must be the fruit of love. His will must be our law because His person is our delight. Some professed believers need to be whipped to their duties. They must hear stirring sermons, attend exciting meetings, and live under pressure. But those who are Christ's friends do not need any spur except love. *"The love of Christ constraineth us"* (2 Cor. 5:14). True hearts do what Jesus asks them to do without having to be flogged and dogged, urged and forced. Coerced virtue is spoiled in the making, as many a piece of earthenware is cracked in the baking. The wine of our obedience must flow freely from the ripe cluster of the soul's love, or it will not be fit for the royal cup. When duty becomes delight and precepts are as sweet as promises, then we are Christ's friends, and not until then.

Those Who Disobey Are Not His Friends

Next, our Lord leads us to conclude from this verse that those who do not obey Him are not His friends. He may still look upon them and be their Friend by changing their hearts and forgiving their sins, but as yet they are not friends of His. A person who does not obey Christ does not give the Savior His proper place, and this is an unfriendly deed. If I have a friend, I am very careful that, if he has honor anywhere, he will certainly have due respect from me. If he is my superior, I am concerned that he should not think that I am intrusive, or imagine that I would take undue advantage of his kindness. My esteem for him will be higher than anyone else's esteem for him. He who is truly Christ's friend delights to honor Him as a great King, but he who will not yield to Him His sovereign rights is a traitor and not a friend.

Our Lord is *"the head over all things to the church"* (Eph. 1:22), and this involves the joyful submission of the members. Disobedience denies to Christ the dignity of that holy headship that is His prerogative over all the members of the body of Christ, and this is not the part of a true friend. How can you be His friend if you will not allow His rule? It is vain to boast that you trust His Cross if you do not reverence His crown.

The person who does not obey Christ's commandments cannot be His friend, because he is not of one mind with Christ—that is evident. *"Can two walk together, except they be agreed?"* (Amos 3:3). True friendship does not exist between those who differ on first principles. There can be no points of agreement between Jesus Christ and the person who will not obey Him, for he in fact is saying, "Lord Jesus, your pure and holy will is obnoxious to me; your sweet and gracious commands are weariness to me." What friendship can there be here? They are not of one mind. Christ is for holiness; this person is for sin. Christ is for spiritual-mindedness; this person is carnally minded. Christ is for love; this person is for self. Christ is for glorifying the Father; this person is for honoring himself. How can there be any friendship when they are diametrically opposed in design, purpose, and spirit? It is not possible.

The person who does not obey Christ cannot be Christ's friend, though he may profess to be. He may claim to be a Christian in a very self-righteous and loud manner, and for that reason he may be all the more an enemy of the Cross. When others see this man walking according to his own lusts, they cry out, *"Thou also wast with Jesus of Nazareth"* (Mark 14:67), and they attribute all his faults to his religion and immediately begin to blaspheme the name of Christ. Our Lord's cause is hindered more by the inconsistent conduct of His professed friends than by anything else.

Suppose you and I had some very close associate who was found drunk in the street or committing burglary or theft—should we not feel disgraced by his conduct? When he is brought before the magistrate, would you like to have it said that this person is your close friend? No, you would cover your face and beg your neighbors never to mention it. For such a person to be known as your friend would compromise your name and character. I say this even weeping, that Jesus Christ's name is compromised and His honor is tarnished among men by many who wear the name of Christian without having the Spirit of Christ. People like this cannot be His dear companions.

The number of wounds that Jesus has received in the house of His friends is grievous. When Caesar fell, he was slain by the daggers of his friends! In trust he found treason. Those whose lives he had spared did not spare his life. Woe to those who, under the appearance of Christianity, *"crucify to themselves the Son of God afresh, and put him to an open shame"* (Heb. 6: 6). Nothing burns Christ's cheek like a Judas kiss, and He has had many such.

Those who do not obey Jesus cannot be owned by Him as His friends, for that would dishonor Him indeed. There was a time—I do not know how it is now—when if any man wanted to be made a count or to get an honorable title, he only had to pay a certain amount at Rome into the papal treasury, and he could be made a noble at once. The titles thus purchased were honorable neither to those who gave nor to those who received them. Whatever His alleged clergy may do, our Lord Himself sells no dignities. The title of "friend of Jesus" is bestowed on those of a certain character, and it cannot be otherwise obtained. His friends are those who obey Him. He grants this title of nobility to all believers who lovingly follow Him, but on His list of friends He enters no others.

Do you not see that His honor requires this? Would you have our Lord stand up and say, "The drunkard is My friend"? Would you want to hear Him say, "That fraudulent bankrupt is My close companion"? Would you want Jesus to claim friendly companionship with the vicious and profane? A man is known by the company he keeps. What would be thought of Jesus if His intimate associates were people of loose morals and unrighteous principles? To go among them for their good is one thing; to make them His friends is another. Where there is no kinship, no likeness, no point of agreement, the fair flower of friendship cannot take root. We may, therefore, also correctly read the text as: "You are not My friends, if you do not do the things that I command you."

Being on Best Terms with Christ

In addition, those who obey Christ best are on the best of terms with Him. "You are My friends," He seems to say, "and you live near Me, enjoying practical, personal friendship and daily communion with Me when you promptly obey." Some of you know by personal experience, my friends, that we cannot walk in holy relationship with Christ unless we keep His commandments. There is no feeling of communion between our souls and Christ when we are conscious of having done wrong and yet are not sorry for it.

If we know that we have erred, as we often do, if our hearts break because we have grieved our Beloved, and if we go and tell Him our grief and confess our sin, we are still His friends. He kisses away our tears, saying, "I know your weaknesses—I willingly blot out your offenses. There is no breach of friendship between us; I will manifest Myself to you still." However, when we know that we are wrong and feel no softening of heart about it, then we cannot pray, we cannot speak with the Beloved, and we cannot walk with Him as His friends. Familiarity with Jesus ceases when we become familiar with known sin. If, again, we know that something is wrong, and we persevere in it, there cannot be any happy friendship between us and our Savior.

If conscience has told you, dear believer, that a certain thing ought to be given up but you continue in it, the next time you are on your knees to pray, you will feel greatly hampered. When you sit down before your Bible and hope to have communion with Christ as you have formerly enjoyed it, you will find that He has withdrawn Himself and will not be found by you. Is it any wonder? If *"sin lieth at the door"* (Gen. 4:7), how can the Lord smile on us? Secret sin will poison communion at the fountainhead. If there is a quarrel between you and Christ and you are hugging closely what He abhors, how can you enjoy friendship? He tells you that sin is a viper that will kill you, but you reply, "It is a necklace of jewels," and you put it around your neck. Do you wonder that because He loves you He is grieved at such mad behavior? Oh, do not bring injury on yourself in this way. Do not pour contempt on His wise commands in this manner.

Some Christians will never get into full fellowship with Christ because they neglect to study His Word and search out what His will is. It ought to be a serious work with every Christian, especially in the beginning of his spiritual walk, to discover what the will of his Lord is on all subjects. Half the Christian people in the world are content to ask, What is the rule of our church? That is not the question. The point is, What is the rule of Christ? Some plead, "My father and mother before me did so." I sympathize to a degree with that feeling. Filial reverence commands admiration. Yet, in spiritual things, we are to *"call no man...father"* (Matt. 23:9), but are to make the Lord Jesus our Master and exemplar. God has not placed your conscience in your mother's keeping, nor has He committed to your father the right or the power to stand responsible for you. Everyone must *"bear his own burden"* (Gal. 6:5) and *"give account of himself to God"* (Rom. 14:12).

Search the Scriptures for yourself, and follow no rule but that which is inspired. Take your light directly from the Sun. Let Holy Scripture be your unquestioned rule of faith and practice. If there is any point about which you are uncertain, I charge you, by your loyalty to Christ, if you are His friend, to try to find out what His will is. Once you are sure on that point, never mind the human authorities or dignities who oppose His law. Let there be no question, no hesitation, no delay. If He commands you, carry out His will, though the gates of hell thunder at you.

You are not His friend, or, at any rate, you are not the kind of friend who could enjoy the friendship, unless you resolutely seek to please Him in all things. The intimacy between you and Christ will be disturbed by sin. You cannot lean your head on His chest, as the Beloved Apostle did (see John 13:23), and say, "Lord, I

know Your will, but I do not intend to do it."
Could you look up into that dear face—that
countenance once so marred, now lovelier than
heaven itself—and say, "My Lord, I love You,
but I will not do Your will completely"? By the
very love He has for you, He will chasten you
for that rebellious spirit if you indulge it. It is a
horrible evil; holy eyes will not endure it. He
"is a jealous God" (Exod. 34:14) and will not
tolerate sin, which is His rival.

*"Ye are my friends, if ye do whatsoever I
command you."* Oh, beloved, see to this! Under
all the crosses and losses and trials of life,
there is no comfort more desirable than the
confidence that you have aimed at doing your
Lord's will. If a man suffers for Christ's sake
while steadily pursuing the course of holiness,
he may rejoice in such suffering. Losses borne
in the defense of the right and the true are
gains. Jesus is never nearer to His friends than
when they bravely bear shame for His sake. If
we get into trouble by our own folly, we feel
the stinging pain in the deepest part of our
hearts. However, if we are wounded in our
Lord's battles, the scars are honorable. For His
sake we may accept reproach and wear it as a
wreath of honor. Jesus delights to be the companion of a person who is cast out by relatives
and acquaintances for the truth's sake and for

fidelity to His Cross. They may call the faithful one a fanatic and an enthusiast and all such ill-sounding names, but there is no need to fret over these things, for the honor of being Christ's friend infinitely outweighs the world's opinion. When we follow the Lamb wherever He goes, He is responsible for the results, not us.

> Though dark be my way,
> Since he is my guide,
> 'Tis mine to obey,
> 'Tis his to provide.

The consequences that follow when we do right belong to God. Abhor the theory that for the sake of a great good you may do a little wrong. I have heard men say, and Christian men, too, "If I were to follow my convictions strictly, I would have to leave a post of great usefulness, and therefore I remain where I am and quiet my conscience as well as I can. I would lose opportunities of doing good, which I now possess, if I were to put into practice all I believe, and therefore I remain in a position that I could not justify on any other ground."

Is this according to the mind of Jesus? Is this your kindness to your Friend? How many bow in the house of Rimmon and hope that the Lord will have mercy on His servants in this thing? (See 2 Kings 5:18.) We will see if it will be so. We may not *"do evil, that good may come"* (Rom. 3:8). If I knew that to do right would shake the whole island of Great Britain, I would be bound to do it. God helping me, I would do it. However, if I heard that a wrong act would apparently bless the whole nation, I would have no right to do wrong on that account. No bribe of supposed usefulness should purchase our conscience. Right is right, and must always end in blessing; wrong is wrong, and must always end in condemnation, though for a while it may wear the appearance of surpassing good.

Did not the Devil lead our first parents astray by the suggestion that great benefit would arise out of their transgression? *"Your eyes shall be opened, and ye shall be as gods"* (Gen. 3:5), said the Deceiver. Would it not be a sublime thing for men to grow to be gods? I can imagine Eve saying, "Certainly, I would not lose the opportunity. The race that is yet to be would blame me if I did. I would not want men to remain inferior creatures through my neglect." For the sake of the promised good she ventured upon evil. Thousands of people sin because it seems so advantageous, so wise, so necessary, so sure to turn out well. Hear what Christ says: *"Ye are my friends, if ye do whatsoever I command you."* If you do evil so that good may come, you cannot walk with Him, but if your heart is set on keeping His words, you will find Him loving you and taking up His abode with you (John 14:23).

Obedience Shows Our Friendship with Christ

Now, by our text we are also taught that the friendliest action a person can do for Jesus is to obey Him. Rich men have thought they were doing the friendliest act possible toward Christ by giving immense sums to build churches or to found orphanages or hospitals. If they are believers and have done these things as acts of obedience to Christ's law of stewardship, they have done well—and the more of such generosity the better—but where splendid charitable donations are given out of ostentation or from the idea that some merit will be gained by the consecration of a large amount of wealth, the whole business is unacceptable. *"If a man would give all the substance of his house for love, it would utterly be contemned"* (Song 8:7). Jesus does not ask for lavish expenditure. He asks us to give ourselves to Him. He has made this the token of true love: *"If ye do whatsoever I command you."*

"To obey is better than sacrifice, and to hearken than the fat of rams" (1 Sam. 15:22).

However much we are able to give, we are obligated to give it, and we should give it cheerfully. But, if we suppose that any amount of giving can serve as a substitute for personal obedience, we are greatly mistaken. To bring our wealth and not yield our hearts is to give the box and steal the jewel. How dare we bring our sacrifice in a leprous hand? We ourselves must be cleansed in the atoning blood before we can be accepted, and our hearts must be changed before our offering can be pure in God's sight.

Others have imagined that they could show their friendliness to Christ by some remarkable action of self-mortification. Among Roman Catholics, especially in the old days, it was believed that misery and merit went together, and so men tortured themselves so that they might please God. They went for many days without washing themselves or their clothes; they mistakenly believed that, in this way, they acquired the odor of sanctity. I do not believe that Jesus thinks a person is any more His friend because he is dirty.

Some put on hair shirts, which made raw wounds. I do not think that the kindly Lord Jesus counts this as a friendly act. Ask any humane person whether he would be gratified by knowing that a friend wore a hair shirt for his sake, and he would answer, "Please let the poor creature wear whatever is most comfortable for him, and that will please me best."

The loving Jesus does not take delight in pain and discomfort; forcing one's body to waste away is no doctrine of His. John the Baptist might have been an ascetic, but certainly Jesus was not. He came *"eating and drinking"* (Matt. 11:19), a man among men. He did not come to demand the rigors of a hermitage or a monastery, or else He never would have been seen at feasts. When we hear of the nuns of St. Ann sleeping bolt upright in their coffins, we take no particular satisfaction in their doing so; a kind heart would beg them to go to bed.

I went through a monastery some time ago, and over each bed was a little cat-o'-nine-tails, which I sincerely hope was used to the satisfaction of the possessor. However, I did not copy the idea and buy a couple for my sons. Neither have I sent one to each of my special friends, for I would never ask them to flog themselves as a proof of friendship. Our Lord cannot be gratified by self-inflicted, self-invented tortures. These things are man-made worship, which is no worship. You may fast forty days if you like, but you will gain no merit by it. Jesus Christ has not demanded this as the gauge of friendship, nor will He regard us as His friends for this. He says, *"Ye are my friends, if ye do whatsoever I command you,"* but He does not command you to starve or to wear sackcloth or to shut yourself up in a cell. Pride invents these things, but grace teaches obedience.

Certain people have thought it would be the noblest form of holy service to enter into a brotherhood or sisterhood. They imagined that they would be truly Christ's friends if they joined the "Society of Jesus." I have sometimes asked myself whether it might not be a good thing to form a league of Christian men, all banded together to live alone for Jesus and to give themselves up entirely and wholly to His work. But, assuredly, the formation of guilds, sisterhoods, or brotherhoods, other than the great brotherhood of the church of God, is something that was never contemplated in the New Testament. You will find no foreshadowing of Franciscans and Dominicans there. All godly women were sisters of mercy, and all Christlike men were of the society of Jesus, but we read nothing of monastic or conventual vows.

Anything that is not commanded in Scripture is superstition. We are to worship God according to *His* will, not according to our wills. Even if I were to consecrate myself entirely to what Roman Catholics called the religious life, by getting away from the associations of ordinary men and trying to spend my whole time in lonely contemplations, there still would be nothing in it, because the Lord Jesus never required it of me. The thing that He does ask is that we will do whatever He commands us.

Why is it that people try to do something that Christ never commanded? A schoolteacher will allow me to use his situation as an example. If he said to a boy in his class, "Now is the time for you to attend to arithmetic," and the boy instead starting practicing his penmanship, would the teacher not ask the boy if he had understood him? If, after a few minutes, he finds the boy writing, does he say, "You have written that line very well"? Not at all. It is a small matter whether the writing has been done well or badly, for to be writing at all when he had been instructed to do his arithmetic is a gross act of insubordination.

It is the same way with you and me. You and I may do something other than Christ's command, and do it splendidly well, and other people may say, "What pious people they are!" But if we do not do the Lord's will, we will not be His friends. We may wear sandals and coarse clothing and renounce boots and coats, but there is no grace in apparel. Excellence lies in doing what Christ has commanded.

Some people think that it is a very friendly act toward Christ to attend many religious services in a consecrated building. They are at morning prayer and evening worship and feasts and fasts without number. Some of us prefer to have our religious services each day in our own homes, and it will be a dreadful thing when family prayer is given up for public services. However, a number of people think very little of family worship; they think they must go to the church or to some other temple made with hands. But let no one dream he is made Jesus' friend in this way.

We are not to forsake *"the assembling of ourselves together, as the manner of some is"* (Heb. 10:25); and it is good for you to meet with God's people as often as you can. Yet, even though you may be multiplying your sacraments and increasing your ceremonies, and may be busy with this service and the other service until your heart is worn away with grinding at the mill of outward religion, you are Christ's friends only if you do whatever He commands you. That is a better test than early communion or daily mass.

It comes to this, dear friends: we must steadily, carefully, persistently, and cheerfully do the will of God from the heart in daily life, from our first waking moment until our eyes are closed. Ask concerning everything: What would Jesus have me do about this? What is the teaching of Christ regarding this? For, *"whether therefore ye eat, or drink, or whatsoever ye do, do all to the glory of God"* (1 Cor. 10:31), and *"whatsoever ye do in word or deed, do all in the name of the Lord Jesus, giving thanks to God and the Father by him"* (Col. 3:17).

You may be a domestic servant and may never be able to give a pound to church work, but you are Jesus' friend if you do whatever He commands you. You may be a housewife and may not be able to do anything outside of the little family that requires all your attention, but if you are fulfilling your duty to your children, doing what Christ commands you, you are among the friends of Jesus. You may be only a plain workingman or a tradesman with a small shop; you may not be well known; but if you set an example of honesty, uprightness, and piety, doing all things as if you were doing them for Christ because He has saved you, He will call you His friend. What title of nobility can equal this? Friendship with Christ is worth a thousand dukedoms.

Live As If Jesus Were Always Present

The practical outcome of all of this is that we must examine every question regarding duty by the light of this one inquiry: Will this be a friendly action toward Christ? If I do this, will I act as Christ's friend? Will my conduct honor Him? Then I am glad. If it will dishonor Him, I will have nothing to do with it. Set each distinct action, as far as you are able, in the scales, and let this be the weight: Is it a friendly action toward my Redeemer?

I wish that we all lived as if Jesus were always present, as if we could see His wounds and gaze into His beautiful countenance. Suppose that tomorrow you are brought into temptation by being asked to do something questionable. Decide what to do in this way: If Jesus could come in at that moment and show you His hands and His feet, how would you act in His sight? Behave as you would act under the realized presence of the Well Beloved. You would not do anything unkind to Him, would you? Certainly you would not do anything to grieve Him if you saw Him before your eyes. Well, keep Him always before you. The psalmist cried, *"I have set the LORD always before me"* (Ps. 16:8).

You will need much of the Holy Spirit's anointing to do this. May God give it to you. Live, dear friend, as if Christ would come at once and detect you in the very act. Do only what you would not be ashamed of if, in the next instant, you should see the Lord sitting on the throne of His glory and calling you before His court. If you live in this way, you will delight in an abundance of peace.

> So shall your walk be close with God,
>   Calm and serene your frame;
> So purer light shall mark the road
>   That leads you to the Lamb.

Obedience will delight you with the blissful presence of your Lord, and in that presence you will find *"fullness of joy"* (Ps. 16:11). You will be the envy of all wise men, for you will be the beloved of the Lord. Your pathway, if it is not always smooth, will be always safe, for Jesus never leaves His friend, and He will never leave you, but will be *"with you alway, even unto the end of the world"* (Matt. 28:20). May this happy condition be yours and mine.

Chapter 6

The Man Who Will Never
See Death

*Verily, verily, I say unto you, If a man keep my
saying, he shall never see death. Then said the
Jews unto him, Now we know that thou hast a
devil. Abraham is dead, and the prophets; and
thou sayest, If a man keep my saying, he shall
never taste of death. Art thou greater than our
father Abraham, which is dead? and the
prophets are dead: whom makest thou thyself?*
—John 8:51–53

In the eighth chapter of John, previous to
the above passage, we hear the Jews, with
malicious voices, assailing our blessed Lord
with this bitter question: *"Say we not well that
thou art a Samaritan, and hast a devil?"* (John
8:48). How very quietly the Savior answers
them! He answers them because He judges

that it is necessary to do so. But He does so
with great patience and with sound argument:
"I have not a devil; but I honour my Father" (v.
49). This is clear proof! No man can be said to
have a devil who honors God, for the evil spirit
from the beginning has been the enemy of all
that glorifies the Father.

Paul, who had not read this passage—for
the gospel of John had not yet been written—
was nevertheless so filled with his Master's
Spirit that he answered in a similar manner
when Festus said, *"Paul, thou art beside thyself; much learning doth make thee mad"* (Acts
26:24). He calmly replied, *"I am not mad, most
noble Festus; but speak forth the words of truth
and soberness"* (v. 25). This was a fine example
of our Savior's gentle and forcible reply: *"I
have not a devil; but I honour my Father."*

My friends, whenever you are falsely ac-
cused and an evil name is hurled at you, if you
must reply, give a *"reason of the hope that is in
you with meekness and fear"* (1 Pet. 3:15). Do
not become heated and hurried, for if you do,
you will lose strength and will be apt to err.
Let your Lord be your model.

The false charge was the occasion of our
Lord's utterance of a great truth. The Jews rush
on, furious in their rage, but He flashes in their
faces the light of truth. To put down error, lift

up truth. Thus, their deadly saying was met by a living saying: *"Verily, verily, I say unto you, If a man keep my saying, he shall never see death."* Nothing baffles the adversaries of the faith as much as uttering the truth of God with unshakable confidence.

The truth that Jesus stated was full of promise; and if they willfully rejected His promise, it became worse to them than a threat. Christ's rejected promises curdle into woes. If these men, when He said to them, *"If a man keep my saying, he shall never see death,"* still went on reviling Him, then their consciences, when afterwards awakened, would have said to them, *"He that believeth not the Son shall not see life; but the wrath of God abideth on him"* (John 3:36). If the believer will never see death, then the unbeliever will never see life. Thus the Gospel itself becomes a *"savour of death unto death"* (2 Cor. 2:16) to those who refuse it, and the very Word that proclaims eternal life threatens eternal death to the willfully unbelieving.

I pray that we may be put into a frame of mind renewed by grace and may be so helped to keep Christ's commands that we may inherit this wondrous promise: *"If a man keep my saying, he shall never see death."* To this end, may the Holy Spirit especially aid me as I first describe the characteristics of the grace-filled believer, the person who keeps Christ's saying. Next, I will dwell on the glorious deliverance of the believer: he will never see death. And then I want to honor the great Quickener. Evidently, according to the Jews in this text, our Lord was making much of Himself by what He said, and, in truth, the fact that the believer will never see death does greatly magnify the Lord Jesus.

Characteristics of Christlike Believers

Consider the characteristics of the grace-filled believer: *"If a man keep my saying, he shall never see death."* Observe that the one conspicuous characteristic of the person who will never see death is that he keeps Christ's saying, or His word. He may have other characteristics, but they are comparatively unimportant in this respect. He may have a timid nature, he may often be in distress, but if he keeps Christ's saying, he will never see death. He may have been a great sinner in his early life, but, because he has been converted and led to keep Christ's saying, he will never see death. He may be a strong-minded person, who keeps a firm grip of eternal realities and therefore is supremely useful, but this promise is none the more true for him, even so. The reason for his safety is the same as it is with the weak and timid person: he keeps Christ's saying, and therefore he will never see death. Divest yourself, therefore, of all inquiries about other matters, and only examine your own heart on this one point: Do you keep Christ's saying? If you do this, you will never see death.

What kind of person keeps Christ's saying? Obviously, he is a person who has a close relationship with Christ. He hears what He says; he notes what He says; he clings to what He says. We meet people nowadays who talk about faith in God, but they do not know the Lord Jesus Christ as the great Sacrifice and Reconciler. Yet, without a mediator there is no coming to God.

Jesus says, *"No man cometh unto the Father, but by me"* (John 14:6). His witness is true. Beloved, we glorify Christ as God Himself. Truly, we never doubt the unity of the Godhead, but while *"there is one God,* [there is also] *one mediator between God and men, the man Christ Jesus"* (1 Tim. 2:5). Forever remember that Christ Jesus, as God-man, as Mediator, is essential to all our communion with the Father. You cannot trust God or love God or serve God in the right way unless you willingly consent to His appointed way of reconciliation, redemption, justification, and access, which is only through the precious blood of Jesus Christ. In Christ we draw near to God. Do not attempt to approach Jehovah, who is *"a consuming fire"* (Heb. 12:29), except through the incarnate God. Tell me, my reader, is your faith fixed on Jesus, whom God has set forth to be the reconciliation for sin? Do you come to God in the way that He has provided? He will not receive you in any other way. If you reject the way of salvation through the blood of the Lamb, you cannot be keeping the saying of Christ. He says, *"He that hath seen me hath seen the Father"* (John 14:9), and He says this of no one else.

Next, the person who keeps Christ's saying, making the Lord Jesus his all in all, reverences His Word and therefore keeps it; he respects, observes, trusts, and obeys it. Keeping His saying means, first, that he accepts His doctrine. Whatever Christ has laid down as truth is truth to him.

My reader, is it so with you? Some people's own thoughts are the chief source of their belief. They judge the divine revelation itself and claim the right not only to interpret it, but also to correct and expand it. In the fullness of self-confidence, they make themselves the judges of God's Word. They believe a doctrine because the light of the present age confirms it or invents it. Their foundation is in man's own thought. In their opinion, parts of Scripture are exceedingly faulty and need tinkering with scientific tools. To them, the light of the Holy Spirit is a mere glowworm compared to the light of the present advanced age.

But the person who is to share in the promise now before us is one who believes the Savior's word because it is His word. He takes the sayings of Christ and His inspired apostles as truth, because he believes in the One who spoke them. To him the inspiration of the Holy Spirit is the warrant of faith. This is a very important matter. The foundation of our faith is even more important than the superstructure. Unless you ground your faith on the fact that the Lord has spoken, your faith lacks that worshipful reverence that God requires. Even if you are correct in your beliefs, you are not correct in your spirit unless your faith is grounded on the authority of God's Word. We are to be disciples, not critics. We are through with quibbling, for we have come to believing.

Next, the grace-filled believer trusts Christ's promises. This is a crucial point. Without trust in Jesus we have no spiritual life. Tell me, my reader, do you rely on this saying of the Lord Jesus, *"Verily, verily, I say unto you, He that believeth on me hath everlasting life"* (John 6:47)? Do you believe in the

promise of pardon to the person who confesses
and forsakes his sin—pardon through the precious blood of the great Sacrifice? Are the
promises of Christ certainties to you, certainties hallmarked with His sacred, *"Verily, verily,
I say unto you"*? Can you hang your soul on
the sure nail of the Lord's saying? Some of us
rest our eternal destiny solely on the truthful-
ness of Christ. When we take all His promises
together, what a fullness of confidence they
create in us!

> How firm a foundation, ye saints of the Lord,
> Is laid for your faith in his excellent word!

Furthermore, the grace-filled believer obeys
His precepts. No person can be said to be keeping Christ's commands unless he follows them,
in practical ways, in his life. Jesus is not only
Teacher, but Lord to us. A true keeper of the
Word cultivates the spirit of love that is the very
essence of Christ's moral teaching. He endeavors to be meek and merciful. He aims at purity
of heart, and peaceableness of spirit. He follows
after holiness, even at the cost of persecution.
Whatever he finds that his Lord has ordained,
he cheerfully performs. He does not rebel
against the Lord's command, thinking that it
involves too much self-denial and separation

from the world, but he is willing to *"enter...in at the strait gate"* (Matt. 7:13) and to follow the *"narrow...way"* (v. 14) because his Lord commands him. Faith that does not lead to obedience is a dead faith and a false faith. Faith that does not cause us to forsake sin is no better than the faith of devils, even if it is very good faith.

> Faith must obey her Father's will,
>   As well as trust his grace:
> A pardoning God is jealous still
>   For his own holiness.

So, now you see what kind of person keeps Christ's words. The person who obeys Jesus' commands receives, through the Word of God, a new and everlasting life, for the Word of God is a living and incorruptible seed, *"which liveth and abideth for ever"* (1 Pet. 1:23). Wherever the seed of the Word drops into soil that accepts it, it takes root, grows, and bears fruit. *"For God so loved the world, that he gave his only begotten Son, that whosoever believeth in him should not perish, but have everlasting life"* (John 3:16). It is by Christ's sayings, or by the Word of God, that life is implanted in the soul. By that same Word the heavenly life is fed, increased, developed, and, at length, perfected.

The power and energy of the Holy Spirit, which work through the Word, are used as the beginning, the sustaining, and the perfecting of the inner life. The life of grace on earth is the blossom, and the life of glory is the fruit. It is the same life all along, from regeneration to resurrection. The life that comes into the soul of the believer when he begins to keep Christ's sayings is the same life that he will enjoy before the eternal throne in the realms of the blessed.

We may know what it means to keep Christ's commands from the fact that He Himself has set us the example. Note well this verse, where Jesus says concerning the Father,

> *Yet ye have not known him; but I know him: and if I should say, I know him not, I shall be a liar like unto you: but I know him, and keep his saying.* (John 8:55)

We are to keep our Lord's sayings, even as He kept His Father's sayings. He lived on the Father's Word, and therefore refused Satan's temptation to turn stones into bread. His Father's Word was in Him so that He always did the things that pleased the Father. When He spoke, He did not speak His own words, but the words of Him who sent Him (John 14:10). He lived so that the divine Word might be carried out completely; even on the cross He took care to make sure that the Scripture was fulfilled. (See John 19:28.)

He said, *"He that is of God heareth God's words"* (John 8:47) and, *"He that hath ears to hear, let him hear"* (Mark 4:9). God's Word was everything to Him, and He rejoiced over His apostles, because He could say of them, *"They have kept thy word"* (John 17:6). He, whose words you are to keep, showed you how to keep them. Live toward Him as He lived toward the Father, and then you will receive the promise He has made: *"Verily, verily, I say unto you, If a man keep my saying, he shall never see death."*

The Glorious Deliverance

Now we turn to the delightful part of our subject, namely, the glorious deliverance that our Lord promises: *"He shall never see death."* Our Lord did not mean that the believer will never die, for He Himself died, and His followers, in long procession, have descended to the grave. Some Christians are comforted by the belief that they will live until the Lord comes and that therefore they will not *"sleep,"* but will only be *"changed"* (1 Cor. 15:51). The hope of our Lord's appearing is a very blessed one, come when He may. However, I do not think that to be alive at His coming is any great object of desire. Is there any real preference in being changed over that of dying? Do we not read that, *"we which are alive and remain unto the coming of the Lord shall not prevent them which are asleep"* (1 Thess. 4:15)? This is a great truth. Throughout eternity, if I die, I will be able to say that I had actual fellowship with Christ in the matter of death and descent into the grave, which those happy saints who will survive will never know. It is not a matter of doctrine, but still, if one could have a choice in the matter, it might be gain to die (Phil. 1:21).

> The graves of all his saints he bless'd,
>   And soften'd every bed:
> Where should the dying members rest,
>   But with the dying Head?

How dear will Christ be to us when, in the ages to come, we will think of His death and will be able to say, "We, too, have died and risen again"! At His coming, you who are alive and remain will certainly not have preference over us, who, like our Lord, will taste death. I am only speaking now of a matter of no great importance, which, as believers, we may use as a pleasant subject of discourse among ourselves.

The Man Who Will Never See Death

Our Lord has said, *"If a man keep my saying, he shall never see death."* This does not mean the few who will remain at His second advent, but to the entire company of those who have kept His Word, even though they have passed into the grave.

We Will Never See Death

What does this promise mean, then? To begin with, it means that our faces are turned away from death. Suppose that here I am, a poor sinner, convinced of sin, and aroused to a fear of wrath. What is there before my face? What am I compelled to gaze on? The meaning of the original Greek verb is not fully interpreted by the word *see* in *"never see death"*: it is a more intense word. According to a noted biblical scholar, the sight mentioned here is that of "a long, steady, exhaustive vision, whereby we become slowly acquainted with the nature of the object to which our vision is directed." The awakened sinner is made to look at eternal death, which is the threatened punishment of sin. He stands gazing on the result of sin with terror and dismay. Oh, the wrath to come! The death that never dies! While I am still unforgiven, I cannot help gazing on it and foreseeing it as my doom.

When the Gospel of the Lord Jesus comes to my soul and I keep His sayings by faith, I am turned completely around. My back is to death, and my face is toward life eternal. Death is removed, life is received, and more life is promised. What do I see within, around, and before me? Why, life, and only life—life in Christ Jesus, *"who is our life"* (Col. 3:4). In my future course on earth, what do I see? Final falling from grace? By no means, for Jesus said, *"I give unto* [My sheep] *eternal life"* (John 10:28). What do I see far away in the eternities? Unending life. *"He that believeth on me hath everlasting life"* (John 6:47). Now I begin to realize the meaning of the verses, *"I am the resurrection, and the life: he that believeth in me, though he were dead, yet shall he live"* (John 11:25) and, *"Whosoever liveth and believeth in me shall never die"* (v. 26).

The person who has received the words of the Lord Jesus has passed from death to life and will never come into condemnation (John 5:24). Consequently, he will never gaze on death. All that lies before the believer is life: *"life...more abundantly"* (John 10:10), life to the full, life eternal (John 17:3). What has become of our death? Our Lord endured it. He died for us. "[He Himself] *bare our sins in his own body on the tree"* (1 Pet. 2:24). In His death, with Him as our representative, we died. There is no death penalty left for the believer, for the least charge cannot be brought against those for whom Christ has died (Rom. 8:33). Therefore, we sing:

> Complete atonement thou hast made,
> And to the utmost farthing paid
>   Whate'er thy people owed:
> Nor can his wrath on me take place,
> If shelter'd in thy righteousness,
>   And sprinkled with thy blood.

Shall *we* die, for whom Christ died in the purpose of God? Can our departure out of the world be sent as a punishment, when our Lord Jesus has so vindicated justice that no punishment is required? When I see my Lord die on the cross, I see that for me death itself is dead.

Free Forever from Spiritual Death

Then there is another meaning to the verse. *"If a man keep my saying, he shall never see death"* means that the person's spiritual death is gone, never to return. Before he knows Christ, he remains in death, and wherever he looks, he sees nothing but death.

Poor souls! You know what I am talking about, you who are anxious about your souls, for you try to pray and find death in your prayers; you try to believe but seem dead regarding faith. I pity you ungodly ones! Although you do not know it, death is everywhere within you. You are *"dead in trespasses and sins"* (Eph. 2:1). Your sins are to you what grave clothes are to a corpse. They seem to be your natural covering; they cling to you; they bind you. Little do you know what corruption is coming upon you, so that God Himself will say of you, "Bury the dead out of my sight."

Yet, just as soon as the Gospel of the Lord Jesus comes to a man with power, what is the effect? He is dead no longer; he begins to see life. It may be that at first it is a painful life: a life of deep regrets for the past and dark fears for the future, a life of hungering and thirsting, a life of pining and panting, a life that lacks something—it scarcely knows what—but cannot live without it. This man sees life. The more he keeps his Savior's words, the more he rejoices in Christ Jesus. The more he rests on His promise, the more he loves Him. The more he serves Him, the more his new life will drive death out of sight. Life now abounds and holds sway, and the old death hides away in holes and corners. Though often the believer has to mourn over the old death that struggles to return, still he does not gaze on that death of sin as he once did. He cannot endure it; he takes no pleasure in the contemplation of it; he cries to God for deliverance from it. Grace frees us from the reign of death as well as from the penalty of death. In neither of these senses will the keeper of Christ's words ever look on death.

"But," someone will cry, "will not a Christian die?" Not necessarily, for some will remain at the coming of our Lord, and these believers will not die. Therefore, there is no legal necessity that any should die, since the obligation would then rest alike on all. Still, good men die. Yet, they do not die as the penalty of their sin. They are forgiven, and it is not according to God's grace or justice to punish those whom He has forgiven.

O my reader, if you do not believe in the Lord Jesus, death will be a penal infliction to you. But the nature of death is changed in the case of believers in Jesus. Our deaths will be a falling asleep, not a going to execution. We will depart out of the world to the Father rather than be driven away in wrath. Through the gate of death, we will leave the militant host of earth for the triumphant armies of heaven. What was a cavern leading to blackness and darkness forever has, by the resurrection of our Lord, been made into an open tunnel, which serves as a passage into eternal glory. As a penal infliction upon believers, death was abolished by our Lord; and now it has become a stairway from the grace-life below to the glory-life above.

Free from the Influence of Death

Christ's word, *"If a man keep my saying, he shall never see death,"* may further mean that the believer will not live under the influence of death. He will not be perpetually thinking of death, dreading its approach and what follows after it. I must admit that some Christians are in bondage through fear of death, but that is because they do not keep their Master's sayings as they ought to. The effect of His words upon us is frequently such that, instead of being afraid to die, we come to the point of longing to depart. In such a case, we should realize the verses of hymn writer Isaac Watts, who tells us that if we could see the saints above, we would long to join them:

How we should scorn these robes of flesh,
    These fetters and this load!
And long for evening to undress,
    That we may rest in God.

We should almost forsake our clay
    Before the summons come,
And pray and wish our souls away
    To their eternal home.

I have to check some dear fellow believers when they say to me, *"Let me die the death of the righteous"* (Num. 23:10). No, do not talk as Balaam did, but rather say, "Let me live, so that I may glorify God and help my sorrowing fellow believers in the Lord's work." I implore you, do not be in a hurry to be gone.

However, this impatience proves that death has lost its terrors for us. We do not see death looming before us as a coming tempest. We do not gaze on it as a fascinating horror that makes our faces pale and casts a lurid glare on all around. We do not see the darkness, for we walk in the light. We do not fear the rumbling of the chariot, for we know Who rides to us in it.

Free from the Wrath of God

In the next place, we will never see that which is the reality and essence of death, namely, the wrath of God in the *"second death"* (Rev. 20:6). We have no cause to fear condemnation, for *"it is God that justifieth"* (Rom. 8:33). That final separation from God, which is the real death of human nature, can never come to us. "[Nothing] *shall be able to separate us from the love of God, which is in Christ Jesus our Lord"* (v. 39)! The ruin and misery that the word *death* describes, when used in relation to the soul, will never befall us, for we will never perish, neither will any pluck us out of Christ's hand (John 10:28).

Free from the Fear of Death

Moreover, when the believer dies, he does not gaze on death. He walks through the valley of the shadow of death, but he fears no evil and sees nothing to fear. A shadow was cast across his road, but he passed through it and scarcely perceived that it was there. Why was that? Because he had his eye fixed on a strong light beyond, and he did not notice the shadow that otherwise would have distressed him. Believers rejoice so much in the presence of their Lord and Master that they do not observe that they are dying. They rest so sweetly in the embrace of Jesus that they do not hear the voice of wailing. When they pass from one world into another, it is something like going from England to Scotland: it is all one kingdom, and one sun shines in both lands. Often, travelers by railway ask, "When do we pass from England into Scotland?" There is no jerk in the movement of the train, no noticeable boundary. Travelers glide from one country into the other and scarcely know where the boundary lies.

The eternal life that is in believers glides along from grace to glory without a break. We grow steadily on from the blade to the ear, and from the ear to the full corn (Mark 4:28), but no line divides the stages of growth from one another. We will know when we arrive, but the passage may be so rapid that we will not see it. Passing from earth to heaven may seem the greatest of journeys, but it ends *"in the twinkling of an eye"* (1 Cor. 15:52).

> One gentle sigh, the fetter breaks,
> We scarce can say, "He's gone,"
> Before the ransomed spirit takes
> Its mansion near the throne.

Believers will never gaze on death; they will pass it by with no more than a glance. They will go through the Jordan as though it were dry land and scarcely know that they have crossed a river at all. Like Peter, departing believers will scarcely be sure that they have passed through the iron gate, which will open of its own accord (Acts 12:10); they will only know that they are free. Of each one of them it may be said, as of Peter, he *"wist not that it was true which was done by the angel; but thought he saw a vision"* (v. 9). Do not fear death, for Jesus says, *"If a man keep my saying, he shall never see death."*

Follow the soul as it enters into the other world: the body is left behind, and the person is a disembodied spirit. However, he does not see death. All the life he needs he has within his spirit by being one with Jesus. Meanwhile, he is expecting that when the trumpet sounds at the Resurrection, his body will be reunited with his spirit, his body having been made to be the dwelling and the instrument of his perfected spirit. While he is absent from the body, he is so present with the Lord that he does not look on death.

But the Judgment Day has come, the Great White Throne is set, the multitudes appear before the Lamb who will judge! What about the keeper of Christ's sayings? Is he afraid? It is the Day of Judgment, the Day of Wrath! He knows that he will never see death, and therefore he is not in a state of confusion. For him there is no, *"Depart from me, ye cursed"* (Matt. 25:41). He can never come under the eternal sentence. See! Hell opens wide its tremendous mouth. The pit, which long ago was dug for the wicked, yawns and receives them. Down sink the ungodly multitude, a very deluge of souls. *"The wicked shall be turned into hell, and all the nations that forget God"* (Ps. 9:17). In that frightful hour, will the believer's foot slip? No, he will *"stand in the judgment"* (Ps. 1:5) and will never see death.

But the world is burning up: all things are being dissolved, and the elements are melting with fervent heat; the stars are falling from heaven like leaves in autumn, and the sun is as black as mourning clothes. Is the believer alarmed now? Ah, no! He will never see death. His eyes are fixed on life, and he himself is full of life. He abides in life; he spends his life praising God. He will never gaze on death, for Jesus says, *"because I live, ye shall live also"* (John 14:19). O blessed eyes that will never look on death! O happy mind that has been made confident in Jesus Christ of an immortality in which there is no danger!

What a glorious word is this! Again, I pity you who are ungodly. You are made to look on death. It haunts you now; what will it be in the hour of your death? What will you do *"in the swelling of Jordan"* (Jer. 12:5)? Nothing remains for you but the wages of sin, which is death. The ruin and misery of your souls will be your endless portion. You will be shut in with the completely destroyed, ruined, and wretched ones forever! This is a dreadful anticipation of judgment. It ought to startle you. But as for the believer, *"surely the bitterness of death is past"* (1 Sam. 15:32). We have nothing more to do with death as a penalty or a terror than we have to do with spiritual death as the

black suffocation of the heart and the mother
of corruption.

Jesus, the Great Quickener

Now, let us move on to rejoice in Jesus as
our great Quickener. Those Jews in the eighth
chapter of John—what a passion they were in!
How unscrupulous was their talk! They could
not even quote Christ's words correctly. They
said, *"Thou sayest, If a man keep my saying, he
shall never taste of death"* (v. 52). He did not
say so. He said, *"Shall never see death."* We
may be said to taste death as our Master did,
for it is written that He *"should taste death for
every man"* (Heb. 2:9). And yet, in another
sense, we will never taste the wormwood and
gall of death (Jer. 9:15), for to us, *"Death is
swallowed up in victory"* (1 Cor. 15:54).
Death's drop of gall is lost in the bowl of victory.

However, the Lord Jesus did not say that
we will never taste death. Neither did He mean
that we will not die, in the common sense of
the word. He was using one of the meanings of
the word *death* that was used by the Hebrew
prophets. The Old Testament Scriptures used
the word *death* or *die* in this way, and these
Jews knew its meaning very well. Death did

not always mean the separation of the soul
from the body, for the Lord's declaration to
Adam was, *"In the day that thou eatest thereof
thou shalt surely die"* (Gen. 2:17). Assuredly,
Adam and Eve died in the sense intended, but
they were not annihilated, nor were their souls
separated from their bodies, for they still remained to labor on earth.

"The soul that sinneth, it shall die" (Ezek.
18:4) relates to a death that consists of degra-
dation, misery, inability, ruin. Death does not
mean annihilation, but something very different. Overthrow and ruin are the death of a
soul, just as perfection and joy are its life forever. The separation of the soul from God is
the death penalty—and that is death, indeed.

The Jews refused to understand our Lord,
yet they clearly saw that what Jesus was
claiming glorified Him above Abraham and the
prophets. Hidden away in their abusive words,
we find a significance that is instructive. It is
not the greatness or the goodness of a believer
that secures his eternal life; it is his being
linked by faith to the Lord Jesus Christ, who is
greater than Abraham and the prophets.

A person keeps Christ's commands, and
this becomes a bond between him and Christ,
and he is one with Christ. Because of their
Lord, the saints live, and the living of the

saints by Him brings glory and honor to Him. His life is seen in every one of His people. Like mirrors, they reflect His divine life. He has *"life in himself"* (John 5:26), and He imparts that life to His chosen. As the old creation displays the glory of the Father, so the new creation reveals the glory of the Son. Believers find the highest life in Christ Jesus their Lord, and every particle of this life glorifies Him.

It is also to our Lord's glory that we live by His Word. He does not sustain us by the machinery of providence, but by His Word. As the world came into being because God spoke, so we live and continue to live because of Christ's words. What He taught, being received into our hearts, becomes the origin and the nourishment of our eternal life. It is greatly glorifying to Christ that, by His Word, all spiritual life in the countless myriads of believers is given birth and sustained.

It is clear that the Lord Jesus is far greater than Abraham and all the prophets. Their word could not make men live, or even themselves live. But the words of Jesus make alive all who receive them. By keeping them, they live—more than this, they live forever. Glory to the name of Him who quickens those whom He wills!

A sweet inference flows from all this, and with it, I conclude: The glory of Christ depends on the fact that all who keep His sayings will not see death. If you and I keep His commands and we see death, then Jesus is not true. If you, believing in Jesus, gaze on death, it will be proved that He did not have either the power or the will to make His promise good. If the Lord fails in any individual case, He has lost the honor of His faithfulness. Oh, you trembling, anxious souls, lay hold of this:

> His honor is engaged to save
> The meanest of his sheep.

If the saint of God, who has won thousands for Jesus, should perish after all, what a failure of covenant obligations there would be! But that failure would be just as great if one of the least of all those who keep our Lord's sayings should be allowed to perish. Such a loss of honor to our all-glorious Lord is not to be imagined. Therefore, if one of you who are the least in your household do really trust in Him—though you are encumbered with infirmities and imperfections—He must keep you from seeing death. His truth, His power, His unchangeable nature, His love—all are involved in His faithfulness to His promise to each believer. I want you to take this to heart and be comforted.

Even if you are some foul transgressor, the greatest sinner who ever lived, if you will come to Christ, lay hold of His gracious words, keep them, and be obedient to them, you will never see death. There is not a soul in hell who can ever say, "I have kept Christ's sayings, and I have seen death, for here I am." There never would be one such as this, or Christ's glory would be tarnished throughout eternity. Keep His commands, and He will keep you from seeing death!